WHO DOES SHE THINK SHE IS?

WHO DOES SHE THINK SHE IS?

BECOMING THE WOMAN I NEEDED
WHEN I WAS A GIRL

by

CeWyon Chandler-Ward

FACET AND FLAME PRESS

Who Does She Think She Is?
Becoming the Woman I Needed When I Was a Girl

© 2026 CeWyon Chandler-Ward

All rights reserved. No part of this book may be reproduced, stored in a retrieval system, or transmitted in any form or by any means, electronic, mechanical, photocopying, recording, or otherwise, without the prior written permission of the publisher, except in the case of brief quotations embodied in critical articles and reviews.

Publisher: Facet and Flame Press
Atlanta, Georgia

This book is a work of nonfiction based on the author's personal experiences and reflections. Some names and identifying details may have been changed to protect privacy.

Paperback Edition ISBN: 979-8-9957446-0-3
Hardcover Edition ISBN: 979-8-9957446-1-0
Ebook Edition ISBN: 979-8-9957446-2-7

Library of Congress Control Number: 2026911847

For the girl I was,
and for every girl who learned to shrink herself just to survive.
May you take your voice back without apology.
Every facet of you is the light.

Acknowledgments

This book tells the story of a woman who spent decades believing she had to carry things alone.

Throughout my life, and throughout the writing of this book, I have been held, championed, encouraged, and loved by more people than these pages could contain. Earth angels who showed up in the right moment with the right word, the right presence, or simply the gift of being there. You know who you are. And I hope you know that I know too.

I could not name you all without writing a second book. But I carry every one of you. Your fingerprints are on this work even if your names are not on this page.

To my beloved brothers, Todd and Cory. No words could ever…

Thank you for being part of the story, even the parts that didn't make it into print.

To my father, James Henry Chandler (February 26, 1936 – July 17, 2021) and my mother, Frankye Marie Grant Chandler (July 22, 1950 – September 5, 2016).

You didn't get to hold this book. I wish you had.

What you did get to hold were my girls, Taylor and Reagan, and for that I am more grateful than I can say. Watching you love them taught me things about how you loved me that I couldn't have understood any other way. Becoming a mother showed me everything.

You gave Toddrick, CeWyon, and Cory all that you had. I know that now. I honor you for it. And I carry you in every page of this.

Reggie.

Thirty-five years ago you walked into my life and stayed. We both did. Not because it was always easy but because we chose to. We have grown together, healed together, and become better versions of ourselves in the presence of each other. You have been my staunch supporter through every version of me, the running one, the shrinking one, the one who was finally still enough to do the work.

You are my family.

Thank you for encouraging me to soar by becoming the string to my kite.

And for allowing me to be the same, for you.

Taylor Simone and Reagan Noelle.

There are not enough pages in this book or any book to say what you mean to me.

You are the reason the healing mattered most. You are the proof that doing the hard work of becoming yourself is not a selfish act, it is the most generous thing a mother can do for her children.

I hope you know that everything I learned to give myself, I learned so I could hand it to you first.

You are my greatest accomplishment. My clearest evidence. My most convincing argument that love, done honestly, changes everything it touches.

I love you both beyond the capacity of language.

Contents

Author's Note

This book is honest. That's the whole point of it.

Some of that honesty includes childhood experiences that may be difficult to read — domestic violence, childhood sexual abuse, and the quiet ways trauma shapes a life before you have words for any of it.

I chose not to look away from them because looking away is what kept me stuck for decades.

If these are your wounds too, take your time. Put the book down when you need to. Come back when you're ready.

I wrote this so you wouldn't have to carry yours alone.

Chapter 1

Kindergarten Dropout

I was four years old, the only brown face in kindergarten.

My brother, Todd, was the only brown face in first grade.

It was English Estates Elementary in Fern Park. In the Orlando area.

If you lined up the whole school by grade, he and I would have been the only two brown faces until at least third grade.

I hadn't landed in that classroom by accident.

I had worked for it.

At four.

When I found out my big brother got to go to school, I made it my personal mission to join him. He was only eleven months older than me. Actually, we were the same age for three days every year, which in my mind made us basically twins separated by a clerical error. If he got a backpack, I needed a backpack. If he got a desk, I needed a desk. If he got to learn things, I needed to learn them too.

I wasn't just tagging along; I was determined.

So when my mother told me I'd have to test into kindergarten early, I treated that exam like the SAT.

I showed up ready.

I showed up focused.

I showed up like a child who already knew the alphabet, the months of the year, the planets, and why Pluto's situation seemed questionable even back then.

I passed.

I got in.

I earned my spot fair and square.

And once I was in the building, I was all in.

I loved learning.

Loved it in that deep, pure way kids do before others make it complicated.

I was excited about everything: reading, writing, numbers, crayons, the smell of new pencils.

I treated my first sight word like it came with prize money.

I wasn't one of those kids who dragged their feet into the classroom.

I practically skipped.

I wanted to learn.

I wanted to ask questions.

I wanted to know why and how and what else.

School was supposed to be my happy place.

A world made of curiosity and discovery.

A world I had fought my way into.

I'd earned my seat.

I wanted my seat.

I needed my seat.

And then I met Mrs. S.

She was the kind of adult who talked to children who looked like me, as if we were unwanted furniture.

Her attitude said rules mattered, her word mattered, and feelings were optional.

Roll call began.

I sat up straight, ready to shine.

I had practiced saying "Present" at home because "Here" was for babies. I was prepared. I was poised. I was waiting for my moment.

"Billy."

"Here."

"Susie."

"Here."

"Kelly."

"Here."

Then she reached my name.

She looked at her paper.

She looked at me.

She looked back at the paper.

"Chew-yon," she said.

A few kids giggled.

This was new entertainment.

I corrected her.

"It's suh-WAHN," I said, hopefully.

She blinked slowly.

Then repeated the wrong version again.

"Chew-yon."

More chuckles.

Round two.

"It's suh-WAHN," I said again. "Salon with a W." (My Mommy had taught me that.)

She stared at me with that irritated grown-woman look meant to remind a child of their place.

By day three, I understood the difference between not knowing and not caring.

Between confusion and contempt.

Between a mistake and a choice.

Every morning she paused at my name, looked straight at me, and dragged out the mispronunciation.

"Siiii-Why-On."

The class would snicker before she even said it.

Some kids practiced it because they thought it was part of the fun.

She never corrected them.

She never said my real name.

She never tried to get it right.

Meanwhile, her own last name was a three-syllable puzzle she pronounced perfectly every time.

Every day I walked into that room excited to learn, and every day roll call reminded me that my name, the first truth I ever owned, was apparently too much.

The shrinking.

The dread.

The humiliation.

Roll call became my enemy.

Every year, every classroom, every teacher.

It followed me through school like a shadow.

I didn't hate my name because of what it meant.

I hated it because of how people handled it.

Something fractured in me in that classroom and stayed broken for decades.

Because when the world keeps mishandling your name, eventually you start mishandling yourself.

That's why, on the morning everything inside me snapped, I didn't ask permission.

I didn't raise my hand.

I didn't wait until recess.

I simply stood up during coloring time, placed my crayon down, picked up my little book bag, pushed in my chair, and walked out.

Not in a tantrum.

Not in a rush.

Just a calm, four-year-old exit.

I walked down the hallway like I belonged to the building.

Reached the front doors.

Pulled them open.

And stepped outside.

Cars passed.

People drove to work.

Everything looked bigger than me, but somehow I wasn't afraid.

I looked both ways like I'd seen adults do.

I waited.

When it seemed safe, I crossed that busy street alone.

I climbed the steps to our place and knocked on the front door like a grown woman who had made a decision.

My mother opened it mid-rush, clearly readying herself for work — her child should be in school, and yet here I stood on the doorstep.

First came shock.

Then fear.

Then fury.

Not at me.

At them.

At the school that hadn't called.

The teacher who hadn't noticed.

The adults who hadn't cared enough to ask where the little Black girl with the hard-to-pronounce name had gone.

"What are you doing here?" she exclaimed.

"I came home," I said, like it was the most obvious thing in the world.

"Why did you leave school, CeWyon?"

I lifted my chin.

"Because Mrs. S. keeps saying my name wrong on purpose. I do not like it there."

That was my whole case.

Four years old.

I had decided the room was disrespectful and left.

A seed had been planted in me that would grow into decades of running.

Leaving opportunities that required my voice.

Leaving rooms that called me everything except who I actually was.

Some people don't struggle with your name.

They struggle with your existence.

I didn't have that language at four years old.

I just knew that something in that classroom felt wrong in a way I couldn't explain, and that my body understood what my words didn't yet have the capacity to say. So I did the only thing that made sense. I removed myself from the situation.

My mother told me never to do it again.

But she also marched herself to that school and made sure nothing like that would happen to me or any other child again.

She was my girl even then.

And I was already, even at four, the child who would evaluate an environment, find it unacceptable, and walk herself out of it. Not in tantrum. Not in tears. In quiet, deliberate decision.

That child never left. She just learned, over years and classrooms and hallways and parking lots, to doubt herself.

This book is about getting her back.

Chapter 2

———————

My Name and I Had Issues

I wish I could tell you that the trouble with my name ended in kindergarten.

It didn't.

If anything, that was just the kickoff.

From that day forward, my name and I developed a complicated relationship.

We weren't enemies, but we definitely weren't friends.

It sat on me like a coat I didn't choose and wasn't sure I looked good in.

People talk about growing into their names.

I grew around mine.

Avoid. Soften. Shorten. Just call me CiCi.

Every year, roll call became a countdown to humiliation.

The pause.

The squint.

The confused inhale.

The inevitable butchering.

The giggles.

I learned to brace myself long before the teacher's mouth got near the C.

At some point, I stopped expecting people to say it right.

Stopped trusting that they would.

Stopped believing my name belonged in the mouths of people who didn't bother to respect it.

And once you stop believing your name deserves to be said correctly, it's a short walk to believing you don't deserve to be fully seen.

That belief followed me farther than any elementary school hallway ever could.

At a young age, I learned the origin story of my name.

My father named me.

And according to him, there really was a girl named CeWyon back in his college days.

I believe she existed.

What I don't believe is that the spelling he handed down survived the journey intact.

Something about it has his creative fingerprint all over it.

Then there was my mother.

She came along more than a decade later, far more evolved than I ever would've been in that situation.

Even if, as my father insists, he and the original CeWyon never dated, I'm not sure I would've been that openhearted.

Not only did she love the name, she added an accent over the e just because she thought it looked elegant.

Completely unnecessary.

Quietly dropped by me the moment I realized it only added more confusion to an already perplexing situation.

And that was that.

My name was set. Official. Permanent.

No one could have predicted that the name both of my parents loved, the one chosen with nostalgia on his side and aesthetic enthusiasm on hers, would become the first thing the world used to make me feel othered.

Over time, I learned how to manage my name the way other kids learned to manage their lunchboxes.

Carefully.

Strategically.

With a plan in place.

Allowing people to say it wrong if correcting them felt like too much work or too much attention.

I'd say it quietly, mumble it, let someone else introduce me, hope the teacher would skip my row, pretend I didn't hear the butchered version so I wouldn't have to fix it in front of everyone.

It wasn't just about the name.

It was about what came after it.

The stillness.

The stare.

The smirk.

Every mispronunciation carried a little message:

You're different.

You're difficult.

You're unfamiliar.

You're a problem to solve.

And when you get that message early enough, for long enough, it starts to settle into your bones.

I began shaping myself around the parts of me that felt easiest for other people.

The friendly part, the funny part, the self-deprecating part, the version of me that didn't challenge or inconvenience anyone.

My name was the first place I learned to dim.

But it wouldn't be the last.

For most of my life, my name arrived before I did.

Not in the good way.

In the way where I'd watch someone's face cloud over the moment they saw it on paper. A flicker of confusion. Sometimes uneasiness. The slight freeze before they attempted it, or decided not to.

I learned to read that look the way some people learn to read weather.

I'd see it coming before they opened their mouths and I'd brace.

I was apologizing for my name before anyone had even asked me to.

Something in me recalibrated. I became a heat-seeking missile for unusual names, attuned to them the way you're attuned to a sound that once hurt you. I noticed them everywhere. And I made it my practice to get them right. Not because I was performing sensitivity. Because I knew, in the most thorough way a person can know something, what it cost to have your name mishandled.

Every person whose name I said correctly, first try, no stumbling, no apologetic grimace, was a small act of repair for something that had been broken in me long before they walked into the room.

The shift didn't come in a single moment.

There was no morning I woke up and decided my name was beautiful. It was more like a slow thaw, the kind you don't notice until you realize the ice has been gone for a while.

The inner work changed me. And my name came along with everything else.

But I remember the moment I knew something had shifted for good.

I was fifty years old.

Someone looked at my name on paper and said it. Correctly. First try. No prompting. No butchering followed by an apologetic recovery.

Just: CeWyon.

I was astonished.

And then I was delighted.

Which told me something. Even after all that work, some part of me had still been tightening. Had still been waiting for the confusion, the freeze, the look.

And then it wasn't necessary.

And somewhere along the way, I learned that two people from my past had given their loved ones my first name. Two others had given loved ones my middle name.

My first instinct, before the healing, would have been horror. Why on earth would anyone do that to a child?

I'm not going to pretend that instinct didn't flicker for just a moment.

But it passed. And what settled in its place was something I hadn't expected.

I was humbled. And genuinely flattered.

The name I had spent decades apologizing for had become someone's gift to a person they loved.

These days, people get it right more often than not. There's a greater sensitivity to names now, a broader understanding that getting someone's name correct is a form of respect. Most people understand that.

And the ones who don't?

I correct them.

Not abruptly. Not with attitude.

Just clearly. With the ease of a woman who knows exactly who she is and what she's called.

My name is CeWyon.

It sounds like salon, but with a W where the L is.

My father gave it to me. My mother added her own flourish. The world spent decades mishandling it.

And I spent decades letting them.

Not anymore.

When it came time to name my own daughters, I knew exactly what I was doing and why.

I wanted names that were distinctive without being burdensome. Gender-neutral, connected to something meaningful, not traditional girl names but not names that would require a lifetime of corrections either. Traditional spellings were non-negotiable. I knew what it meant to spend a lifetime spelling yourself for other people.

Taylor came first. I had always loved that name. It also connected two families, my husband Reggie and me, because Taylor is his mother's and stepfather's last name. Simone came because I had always loved it, always wished it had been mine. Together they became Taylor Simone.

Reagan came from an unlikely place. I was watching *The Exorcist*, through my hands, eyes barely open, when I caught the main character's name. Regan. I loved the sound of it instantly, and Reagan, with the extra A, felt like the right version for my girl. Noelle came at the suggestion of a dear friend and neighbor. We thought they went beautifully together. I cleared the name with another dear friend whose daughter had the same name, spelled differently, out of respect. She was gracious. So Reagan Noelle came to be.

Decades later, Reagan's name still makes me smile. Close enough to Reggie. Matching Taylor's energy. Traditional spelling. Every box checked.

Before I had daughters of my own, my younger brother Cory and his wife honored me with something I still can't fully put into words. They allowed me to name their first daughter.

Honored isn't a big enough word, actually.

A woman who had spent decades apologizing for her own name was trusted to give someone else's child theirs.

I named her Jai Simone. Cory changed the spelling to Cymone. Over twenty years later, Jai honored me by choosing a name I had recommended for her own daughter.

Kendall Sanaa.

That is what it looks like when a wound becomes a gift.

Even with all that shrinking, there was still something in me that refused to disappear completely.

Call it spirit, grit, stubborn brilliance.

Whatever it was, it kept rising to the surface whether I invited it or not.

I could dim myself, but I could never fully turn myself off.

Teachers noticed me even when I tried to stay in the safe middle.

Adults tapped me for things I didn't sign up for.

I'd get chosen to lead, chosen to speak, chosen to represent, all while I was trying not to become a target.

On the inside, I felt unsure.

On the outside, I kept being called into spaces built for someone sure of herself.

Looking back, I can see it clearly:

my power never agreed to the terms of my shrinking.

It kept leaking out in ways I couldn't control.

Through my ideas, my presence, my competence, my ability to connect with people, even the way I walked into a room.

No matter how much I tried to manage myself, something in me kept tapping the glass, saying,

"I'm still here."

By adolescence, that tug-of-war had settled into its own rhythm.

I wasn't trying to hide.

I sat in the front.

I paid attention.

I showed up fully.

I just didn't want extra attention.

Because extra attention came with commentary.

Especially this one:

"Who does she think she is?"

I heard it in hallways, in whispers, in passing.

Sometimes directed at me, sometimes sent sailing just loud enough to land.

And every time, I'd think,

"I don't think I'm anybody. I'm just me."

I didn't think I was cute.

I didn't think I was special.

I had the same insecurities everyone else did.

Big lips I hadn't learned to love.

Skinny bird legs I prayed would fill out.

A face I wasn't sure how to feel about.

I wasn't walking around with big energy.

I was walking around trying not to offend anyone with my existence.

But people project onto what they notice, and I was noticeable even when I didn't try to be.

Not because I thought I was somebody.

But because I was carrying a light I didn't yet understand.

So I moved through adolescence in that strange middle place —
standing out whether I wanted to or not,

and still trying to make myself small enough not to provoke resentment.

I wasn't hiding.

I was navigating.

Balancing.

Trying to survive being myself.

I kept getting opportunities I didn't ask for.

Roles I hadn't applied for.

Compliments I didn't trust.

Responsibilities I didn't feel ready for.

The world kept calling me forward.

And I kept asking,

"Are you sure you meant me?"

The more I tried to manage how much of myself to show,
the more life kept trying to hand me the microphone.

It would take me years to understand why.

Years to see the pattern.

Years to realize that the thing I spent most of my life tiptoeing around, my voice, was the one thing I was never meant to hide.

Chapter 3

My Résumé Looked Like Witness Protection Paperwork

I chose my first college major because the line was shortest at my high school career fair.

When they said I could make around thirty thousand dollars a year, I said, "Sign me up," without much thought about whether I actually wanted to be a physical therapist.

I enrolled at Howard with plans to apply to PT school after the prerequisites.

And when I realized it was not for me, I pivoted.

That was the beginning of understanding that passion does not always have to lead your paycheck.

Sometimes you do what you are good at, and you build your joy elsewhere.

Some folks have a five-year plan.

I had a "leave before I'm exposed as unqualified" plan.

And it worked.

A little too well.

By the time I reached adulthood, I had turned reinvention into a reflex. Not intentionally. But because every time life nudged me toward my actual calling, I sidestepped and sprinted in a different direction. If confidence felt risky, reinvention felt safe. So while other people followed career paths, I followed escape routes.

I tried almost everything.

I was a licensed insurance agent.

I was a firefighter. No, that's not a typo.

I was a Fortune 50 IT Business Analyst, too.

At one point, it felt like I was trying on careers the way some people try on outfits, hoping something would finally fit.

If the role allowed me to be excellent without forcing me to trust that I belonged there, I tried it.

My résumé looked like I was either running from the law or collecting material for the memoir I didn't know I'd one day write.

And here's the crazy part.

I excelled at almost all of it.

Not because I loved it or because it fulfilled me.

Because excellence was my camouflage.

If I performed flawlessly, maybe no one would notice I didn't feel as smart or capable as they assumed. If I delivered more than required, no one would question whether I was the right choice. If I stayed ahead, no one would see how deeply I doubted myself.

Everyone else looked solid. I felt like the exception.

People say, "You can't outrun your purpose."

I disagree.

You can outrun it for years.

Through promotions, new titles, new jobs, clean exits, and glowing references.

You can outrun it right into burnout.

What you can't outrun is the moment you finally get still.

And I wasn't ready for stillness yet.

Not even close.

I had more running to do.

Before my spa franchise. Before the lease and the vision board and the two-handed signature.

Before I understood any of what I'm about to tell you.

There was a job.

Not a good job or a respectable job or a job that looked impressive on paper.

The job. The one that sat at the exact intersection of everything I was made for: performing arts, fine arts, business, young people, purpose.

I was Senior Program Director at Usher's New Look Foundation.

The foundation serves youth from disadvantaged backgrounds. The main product was a two-week camp, immersive, intensive, transformative. Students developed their talents around dance, acting, music, or television production. And because it all centered on Usher's world, everything we built creatively was tied to what was happening in his professional life in real time.

When he partnered with an international brand to create a cologne, their representatives walked me through the process, the brand, the vision. I took what they shared and built a curriculum around it. Students didn't just study the product, they created their own. They learned the business of music, the business of branding, the business of turning talent into something that could sustain a life.

When the foundation was invited to partner with the United Nations and the Captain Planet Foundation on the Nothing But Nets program to fight malaria, their teams brought me into their world the same way. I took what I learned and built curriculum from it. Students designed full marketing campaigns using their talents. They composed and performed original jingles. They shot their own PSAs. I didn't just develop the curriculum. I taught it. And I trained the trainers to do the same.

Everyone had a nickname at camp. Usher's was Big Brother Almighty.

Mine was Biz Mark C.

I didn't come up with it. The students did. A play on Biz Markie, the rapper known for "Just a Friend." They saw something in me and named it before I could argue with them about whether it fit.

It fit.

It still does. To this day, when I run into one of them, that's what they call me.

The work that stays closest to my heart happened through a partnership with the Annie E. Casey Foundation. They brought together approximately 400 foster care youth from across the country, all of them close to eighteen, all of them on the brink of aging out of a system that had been their whole world and would soon release them into a life they'd have to build entirely alone.

I developed a life skills curriculum around the person they wanted to become.

Not who the system said they were. Not what their circumstances suggested they could be.

Who they wanted to be.

They explored every dimension of that person. Then they mapped the behaviors, the mindsets, the resources, the steps. They built a bridge from where they were standing to where they wanted to go.

I can still see their faces.

The smiles. The twinkle in their eyes when the realization arrived, not when Usher walked in, though that produced its own particular electricity, but when they understood that the person they wanted to become wasn't as far away as they'd believed.

I did that.

The curriculum did that.

I was in a room with hundreds of young people who had been failed by nearly every system designed to protect them, and I showed them that who they wanted to be was already inside them, closer than their fear had told them.

I couldn't feel what I was building.

I was mapping the distance for children who couldn't see how close they were, while being completely unable to see it for myself.

That's the particular cruelty of impostor syndrome. It doesn't announce itself. It just stands quietly in the corner of every room you're lighting up and whispers: any minute now.

Any minute now, someone was going to figure out that I didn't know what I was doing.

That voice. That same voice from every room I'd ever half-inhabited, every opportunity I'd half-accepted, every door I'd redirected before it could fully open.

My schedule was demanding in the way that dream jobs sometimes are, consuming, all-in, constantly calling. Rare were the mornings I got to take my daughters to school. So when one of those mornings arrived, I was thrilled. Present. Grateful for the ordinary gift of it.

I pulled into the parking lot of my youngest daughter's Montessori school.

And I noticed the other children.

They were dressed in their Sunday best. Little dresses. Polished shoes. Hair done with intention.

My daughter was in her regular school clothes.

I didn't know what she should be wearing that morning.

Not because I'd missed a newsletter or forgotten to check a calendar.

Because I had been so far from the ordinary rhythm of her life that I didn't know. Couldn't have known. The daily details of her world, what day was special, what that day required of her, what she was supposed to look like when she walked through those doors. I had become a stranger to all of it.

Inside, I learned it was Tea Day.

The children dressed up. Attended a special outing. High tea.

I stood there in that school and knew.

Her big sister was starting middle school that year. A time when girls need their mothers close, present, paying attention. And I was two weeks at a stretch in someone else's world, building curricula around someone else's dreams, pouring into someone else's children.

I resigned the next week.

I told myself it was for them. And part of it was. The love for my daughters was real. The grief of that parking lot was real.

The love made the decision make sense. The fear made me leave.

I'd been waiting for the moment someone walked into my office, looked at everything I'd built, and said: we think there's been a mistake.

Tea Day gave me an exit that felt like sacrifice instead of retreat.

And I took it.

I was made for that role. I knew it then and I know it now. The people around me knew it too. They said so, repeatedly, in ways I cataloged and immediately discounted.

I just didn't believe it.

I left before anyone could prove me wrong.

And I called it love.

I tell this story all the time.

In my speeches. To rooms full of people standing at the same cliff I walked off. I tell them:

Don't let you stop you. Get out of your own way.

I just haven't sought out the specific conversation with the people who were in that room with me. Not the colleagues. Not Usher, whom I've run into since. He's always gracious. We've spoken. The last time, at a football game at the school our children both attended, the moment almost presented itself.

But the sidelines are not the place for a conversation like that.

The story belongs to whoever needs it. Right now, it belongs to every person who has ever talked themselves out of a room they were made for.

It belongs to you.

The first identity I tried on was the "responsible young woman who has her life together."

It wasn't glamorous.

It wasn't thrilling.

It was safe.

People reward responsibility. Responsibility doesn't require vulnerability. It doesn't require you to believe in yourself. It just requires you to do everything right.

So I put that identity on like a pressed uniform.

Reliable, prepared, professional.

The girl who could be trusted with anything because she would get it done.

Responsibility felt like a shield.

If I was dependable enough, maybe no one would notice that underneath the competence, I felt unsure.

Not incapable.

Just… less than.

Like everyone else had a manual I didn't get.

At first, the responsible identity fit.

But over time, it felt tight in all the wrong places.

I was functioning, not flourishing.

Achieving, not aligning.

Busy, not lit up.

It was like working overtime in a life that didn't actually belong to me.

But I stayed.

Paper mattered more than peace.

I wasn't avoiding success. I was avoiding being exposed.

When you grow up shrinking your identity to avoid attention, adulthood becomes a continuation of the same survival strategy: better outfits and W-2s.

Responsibility wasn't my calling, but it was my cover.

So I reinvented myself again.

If my twenties were a movie, the title would've been:

"New Job, Who This?"

Some people explore hobbies.

I explored entire careers.

I was always the new hire learning a new world, adapting at lightning speed, proving myself from day one.

People praised my versatility.

My quick learning, my leadership qualities, my initiative.

They never saw the part where I went home every night wondering when someone would figure out I wasn't as naturally talented as they believed.

Insecurity could wear a professional outfit and call itself "prepared."

I just assumed everyone else felt comfortable and I was the only one who didn't belong.

Every time a job needed more of my voice —

more presence, more opinion, more truth —

I felt something tighten.

Not because I couldn't do it.

But because I didn't understand why I'd been chosen.

So I left before anyone could "find me out."

A graceful exit neatly wrapped around a quiet fear.

But no matter how many times I tried to reinvent myself, opportunities kept finding me. My gifts kept showing up before I could hide them.

I'd get tapped, promoted, recommended, chosen.

To the outside world, it looked like ambition.

To me, it felt like trying to outrun a spotlight that kept tracking me even in the dark.

It took a long time before I connected the dots.

Long enough to accumulate titles, experiences, and a résumé that didn't match my internal world at all.

Every escape had the same trigger:

Whenever a role required my full brilliance,

my full capacity, my full voice, my full truth,

I ran.

Not because I lacked ability.

Because I doubted the legitimacy of my own talent.

I didn't fear leading.

I feared being seen as an accident.

A misunderstanding. An overestimation.

I just knew I didn't feel as smart, as capable, or as deserving as people made me out to be.

But the truth doesn't disappear.

It waits. Patiently.

And eventually, every path I tried led me back to the same realization:

You can outrun a lot of things,

but you cannot outrun who you are.

And who I was —

who I am —

was starting to break through every mask I put on.

Chapter 4

The Lunch That Changed Nothing...Until It Changed Everything

I walked into that lunch like it was nothing more than a midday hangout with an old undergrad classmate.

No nerves.

No expectations.

No performance mode.

Just me, my purse, and the promise of good food.

He'd invited his friend, someone I already knew of and respected, but it wasn't that kind of lunch.

I wasn't pitching myself.

I wasn't angling for anything.

I wasn't trying to be impressive.

We were three adults at a table, eating and laughing like people do when life has taken them in different directions but the vibe still works.

It was light.

Easy.

Comfortable.

Then my friend — bless him — casually mentioned my work with Usher's nonprofit.

Work I had quietly walked away from years earlier.

Work I had minimized in my mind, even though it had clearly made a stronger impression on everyone else.

Before I could swallow my next bite, the friend-of-the-friend leaned in a little, nodded like he'd just connected a dot, and said:

"Viola Davis wants to start a foundation.

She needs someone like you.

We could recommend you."

Just like that.

Like he was asking if I wanted dessert.

Like being connected to Viola Davis was a regular Tuesday opportunity.

My smile didn't move.

My posture didn't shift.

But inside, everything in me dropped three floors.

My inner voice didn't whisper.

It screamed.

"Who are you to work with her?"

"Don't freeze — look normal."

"Quick, quick, QUICK — redirect!"

"You cannot let them find out you don't really know what you're doing."

"All those compliments?

Girl, they were just being polite."

Meanwhile, my actual body?

Sitting there like I was discussing the weather.

Not a twitch.

Not a blink.

Olympic-level composure.

Inside, though, I was mentally drafting exit strategies like:

"Is there a polite way to fake a phone call?"

"Do I spill water on myself and pretend I need to leave?"

"Can I dramatically clap my hands and shout, 'Actually, I know someone PERFECT for that!'"

And that's exactly what I did, not the clap, but the redirect.

I redirected him to someone else so fast you would've thought he'd offered me the role outright instead of simply the chance to be considered for it.

That's the part that still gets me.

He hadn't offered me the job.

He was the person with Viola Davis's ear —

directly, personally, already in her world —

and he was offering to put my name in it.

Not through a chain of connections.

Not a long shot referral into the void.

A door held open by the man standing right in front of it.

And I didn't even let it get that far.

Didn't allow myself to take a meeting.

Didn't give Viola Davis, or myself, the chance to find out.

I pre-rejected myself before anyone else had the chance to weigh in.

Pointed him toward someone more deserving

before Viola Davis could decide for herself whether I was.

It wasn't dramatic.

It wasn't suspicious.

It was a smooth, benign little pivot —

a masterclass in polite self-sabotage.

All on the outside?

Calm.

Poised.

Professional.

But inside?

My spirit was in the restroom gripping the sink asking,

"What is happening right now?"

Lunch wrapped up like nothing had happened.

We hugged, said our goodbyes, and laughed in the parking lot.

It wasn't until I got in the car that the truth caught me.

I closed the door and everything went still. Not quiet. Still. The way a vacuum is still — like sound itself had left.

My stomach dropped. Heavy in a way that had nothing to do with lunch. I didn't move. Just sat there while something I'd been holding for years finally stopped holding.

And then the tears came. Not cute ones. Not misty-eyed reflection. The kind that come from the oldest place in you — the place that's just had it.

I cried out to God right there in that car. No soundtrack. No dramatic pause. Just my voice, breaking:

"Why do I keep closing the doors You open? What's wrong with me?"

When I got still enough to listen, something shifted.

I'd been asking the wrong question.

Not what's wrong with me.

What happened to me.

Not because it had an easy answer. It didn't. But because it was finally the right question. The one that pointed toward understanding instead of verdict. The one that treated me like a human being who had been shaped by her experiences rather than a character flaw walking around in a woman's body.

What's wrong with me assumes the answer lives inside a defect.

What happened to me assumes the answer lives inside a story.

And stories can be understood. Examined. Reframed. They don't have to define you. They just have to be told honestly.

I sat in that car for a long time after the tears passed. Not numb. Not empty. Something closer to the feeling after a storm when everything is quiet and the air smells different and the light looks different and you understand that something has changed even if you can't name exactly what.

Something had changed.

I didn't know yet how far back it all went or how much of it I had been carrying without knowing it had a name.

I just knew that the question had changed.

And that was enough to begin.

Chapter 5

Disappearing Night

My earliest memories are not of bedtime stories or Saturday morning cartoons or the smell of breakfast on a slow morning.

My earliest memories are of fighting.

Not the quiet, tense kind that lives behind closed doors and polite smiles.

The kind that spilled into daylight.

Into driveways.

In front of neighbors who watched from windows and doorways

and then went back inside

and never said a word.

I remember being scooped up —

a toddler, my brothers beside me, one still an infant —

carried out of the house in the middle of an argument

and placed in my father's car.

Before he left, my mother threw his slippers down the stairs.

He was taking her babies in the middle of an argument, using them as the final word in a fight she had dared to start.

She was furious.

She was powerless.

And the only agency she had left in that moment, the only thing still in her hands, was his comfort.

And she chose it anyway.

Because that's who she was.

Even being punished for expecting better, even watching her children loaded into his car in the dark — at least his feet won't be cold.

That gesture has lived in me for fifty years.

The contradiction of it.

The tenderness inside the chaos.

The way love and pain can occupy the same breath,

the same staircase,

the same pair of slippers.

We ended up at the home of whoever he was seeing at the time.

His children and hers, arranged on a pallet in front of a television

while the adults disappeared into another room.

Nobody asked if we were okay.

Nobody explained what was happening.

We just watched whatever was on the screen

and waited to be taken home.

This was not a single incident.

This was the weather of my childhood.

Not an interruption to the childhood.

The childhood.

There was no before.

No golden period that the fighting interrupted.

No safe baseline I was trying to get back to.

The calibration, the reading of rooms, the managing of temperature, the practice of looking fine, didn't begin at Maitland.

It began here.

On a pallet.

My parents loved fiercely.

They fought fiercely.

Sometimes in the same breath.

And the community that watched it happen in broad daylight —

the same neighbors who saw the car, the children, the slippers on the stairs —

chose to look away.

We were, by most accounts, an admired family.

High achieving. Put together. The kind of family people pointed to.

And so people pointed.

And looked away from everything else.

Inside, I was the one who jumped in.

Not because anyone asked me to.

Not because I had any power to stop anything.

But because I couldn't not.

I would plant myself between them —

a child, small enough that this was almost absurd —

and I would get sent back to my place.

Stay in a child's place.

That's your father. You need to respect him.

I understood the word respect.

I didn't understand how to apply it to what I was watching.

No one explained that.

No one explained any of it.

And then my mother would come to me —
not to reassure me,
not to explain,
but to process.
To tell me what he'd done.
And then, in the same breath,
tell me not to hate him for it.
Don't resent your father.
And he would tell me himself —
calm, matter-of-fact, almost proud of his own honesty —
Your mother knew I was no good when she met me.
I'm gonna be no good till I die.
I was a child being handed information I had no container for.
Feelings I was not permitted to feel.
How can I respect what isn't respectable?
I never said it out loud.
But I thought it.
And then I learned not to think it.
Because thinking the wrong things had consequences too.
So I became what the situation required.
I became the adjuster, the calibrator, the one who read the room before entering it, who managed the temperature before it rose, who held herself together because falling apart was a luxury the house couldn't afford.
We were taught not to look like what we were living.
And we were very, very good students.
Later, years later in high school, I would fall asleep in my afternoon classes.
Every day. Reliably.
Not because I was bored.

Because I was exhausted.
Because some nights were spent mediating.
Because some mornings I'd helped my mother tend to herself
before I packed my bag and walked out the door
looking like everything was fine.
Not one teacher asked why.
Not one adult in that building —
or in that neighborhood,
or in that community that had watched us for years —
ever pulled me aside and said:
Hey. Are you okay in there?
Maybe they didn't know what to do with the answer.
Maybe the family's image made the question feel impolite.
Maybe it's easier to let a child fall asleep at her desk
than to open a door you're not sure you want to walk through.
I don't know.
What I do know is that I learned,
in the way only a childhood can teach you,
that you can be in plain sight
and still be completely invisible.
That you can be admired from the outside
and utterly alone on the inside.
That the people who are supposed to ask
sometimes never do.
And that a child who never gets asked
eventually stops expecting to be seen.
She just gets better at looking fine.
Which is why, by the time I reached middle school,
I was already fragile in ways I hadn't admitted to myself.
The walkway at Maitland Junior High School
wasn't the beginning of anything.

It was the final crack
in a foundation that had been weakening
for as long as I could remember.
At school, I never quite fit.
At home, there was no version of fit available to me.
There was no place, not one,
where I felt fully safe or fully seen.
So by the time this day happened,
I was already carrying more than any child should carry.
And then came the moment that broke me open.
I was walking down the long outdoor walkway between classes,
book bag swinging,
trying to stay invisible,
when I saw the group up ahead —
boys and girls huddled together,
laughing too loudly,
watching me approach with a certain kind of anticipation.
Not strangers.
Kids I knew.
Kids I had laughed with.
Kids who should have been safe.
As I got closer, one boy lit up like he'd been waiting for his
cue.
"Hey, did y'all see CeWyon on TV?
This is how she dances!"
He broke into a clumsy, off-key chant
and threw himself into an exaggerated leap —
arms wild, legs everywhere —
a cruel caricature of me.
The group erupted.
Laughter.

Pointing.
Delight at my expense.
And walking toward them, with no way around,
my mind snapped into survival mode:
Smile.
Stay calm.
Keep walking, CeWyon.
You'd better not let them see you cry.
As I passed,
the girl who bullied me most
leaned in just loud enough to hit the center of my chest:
"She thinks she's so cute.
I'm gonna beat her up after school."
I kept walking.
Didn't look at her.
Didn't flinch.
Didn't speed up or slow down.
But something inside me collapsed.
I made it to the restroom
before the tears finally escaped.
I didn't just feel hurt. I felt gutted. These were my people —
we had grown up together.
This moment wasn't isolated. Our dynamic had changed.
The jokes had started to land differently. What used to feel
like playing around started to carry an edge.
Junior high expanded everything — activities, visibility, new
groups forming around shared interests. I was moving in spaces
that didn't naturally include them, while still moving in the
spaces we had always shared. I moved between both with ease.
What felt like expansion to me didn't feel neutral to them.
I felt like I was growing. They seemed to think I was leaving.

I slipped into the last stall,
shut the door,
and folded my legs under me.
Then I pulled out my notebook
and wrote a song.
Not a pretend song.
A real one.
"I live a life
where there are no pleasures.
I have no friends.
I'm. All. Alone."
The melody is still somewhere in my memory.
Not off-key.
A plaintive wail.
The kind a girl sings when she has nowhere else to put the truth.
I was a singer.
I knew what I was doing.
Later, I set it to the Art of Noise's "Moments in Love," that slow, aching instrumental that already sounded like grief with nowhere to go, and sang it in chorus.
I loved that song from the moment I heard it. Beautiful. Haunting. The kind of melody that begs for words. I didn't fully understand yet how dark the words I'd given it were. I just knew it held something I couldn't say any other way.
I would dance to it too — take it onto a real stage, a solo, just me and that song — and that someone watching would change the course of my life.
But that comes later.
My chorus teacher heard it.
She paused.

The same way the song does.
Said it was sad.
And said nothing more.
I have never forgotten that pause.
Or that silence.
I walked through the rest of the day numb.
And that night,
the numbness thickened into something heavier.
Because it wasn't just the walkway.
It wasn't just the mocking.
It wasn't just the threat.
It was everything —
the loneliness at school,
the loneliness at home,
the feeling of not belonging anywhere.
The feeling that the world had no place carved out for me.
And in that darkness,
I reached a conclusion no child should ever reach.
I decided I didn't want to be here anymore.
I wrote a goodbye letter
and slid it under my parents' bedroom door.
But I didn't sleep.
I couldn't.
Even in my pain,
I thought of my two brothers —
how they would wake up shattered.
How they would carry that weight forever.
So before morning,
I got up,
walked quietly down the hallway,
retrieved the letter,

and tucked it away.
No one ever knew.
But everything changed.
A belief rooted itself inside me that night —
quiet, heavy, absolute:
Don't give people anything they can use against you.
Don't shine too brightly.
Don't love anything too loudly.
Hide what matters most.
Hide what brings you joy.
Hide yourself.
I didn't disappear.
But a part of me did.
The part that felt safe anywhere.
The part that trusted freely.
The part that believed belonging was guaranteed
and not something I had to earn.
This was not the beginning.
The beginning came long before this hallway,
long before this school,
long before a boy mocked my dancing
and a girl threatened me after class.
The beginning was a pallet on a stranger's floor.
A pair of slippers on a staircase.
A community that watched and went back inside.
But this —
this walkway,
this bathroom,
this night —
was the moment everything that had been quietly breaking
finally broke all the way through.

The day I didn't disappear —

but felt hopeless enough to believe I should.

The next morning was a Saturday.

I know because of the music.

My mother had a ritual for Saturday mornings. The radio went on, not softly, not as background, on. The kind of volume that fills a house from corner to corner, that finds you wherever you are and pulls you into its current whether you meant to be pulled or not.

And we cleaned.

That was the deal. The music played and we moved through the house, all of us, doing what needed doing, putting things back in order. It was structure. It was routine. It was, I understand now, its own kind of medicine.

That particular Saturday, the radio was doing what Orlando radios did in 1985. Whitney Houston. Deniece Williams. The R&B chart-toppers that everyone knew because they were simply in the air that year, inescapable, unavoidable, woven into the fabric of ordinary life.

When "Saving All My Love for You" came on, we belted it.

All of us. At the top of our lungs. Every word.

And then my mother put on Deniece Williams.

The whole *My Melody* album. On repeat. The way she did on mornings like that one, those exact mornings, the ones after the hard nights, the ones where everyone had to get up and look like everything was fine.

We knew every word of that album. Every song. We knew it the way you know something that has been played enough times to become part of your body, something you carry without deciding to carry it.

When "Silly" came on, we got animated.

That's the only word for it. Something in that song reached in and pulled something out of us, the grief, the tension, the weight of whatever the night before had been, and for three minutes and however many seconds, we were just kids in a house, singing a song about love, exaggerating every note, performing for each other and for no one.

Music could do what words couldn't.

After a hard night, when everything in me felt off-kilter, it was melody and rhythm that brought me back to something I could hold. The beat in your chest when you sing loud enough.

I just knew the music was playing.

And I let it carry me.

The way it always had.

The way, I would eventually understand, my body had always known it needed to be carried.

Chapter 6

The Rules I Learned Without Knowing I Learned Them

After that day at Maitland Junior High School —
the walkway, the laughter, the threat, the bathroom stall,
the letter I retrieved before sunrise —
I didn't wake up a different girl.
I woke up a girl who had learned different rules.
Rules no one spoke out loud.
Rules no adult sat down to teach me.
Rules that slipped under my skin quietly,
the way old pain becomes new behavior.
Maitland wasn't where these rules were born.
They were already in me.
Maitland just made them permanent.
The first rule was simple:
Don't give anyone something they can use against you.
So I stopped offering pieces of myself freely.
My joy, my excitement, my dreams, the things that lit me up.
I kept them small, private, protected.

I had learned this one at home first.

In a house where feelings were dangerous, where honesty could escalate, where love could turn on itself in the same breath, you kept the tender things out of reach.

It had happened before the Bullets. Before Howard. Before any of it.

I was about fifteen, dancing at Miss Black Orlando — not competing, performing. Part of the entertainment between competition segments. I danced a solo that night, my "Moments in Love" piece. Just me and the song. Afterward, a woman approached me.

"Have you ever modeled?" she asked.

"Yes," I said. "Local fashion shows. Nothing major."

Dimming it before she could. Already.

She didn't flinch. She worked for Revlon. She wanted me to travel to Miami to model for their Realistic hair care line.

I said yes.

I traveled. I worked. I saved.

When I told my guidance counselor at Edgewater High School I had chosen an HBCU, she looked at me like I had announced something reckless.

She said, "Why would you do that when you could probably get into any school, based on your test scores?"

She had only called me into her office once that year. She mispronounced my name. And somehow, in that moment, felt confident questioning one of the most important decisions of my life.

I left her office feeling small, not because I doubted my choice, but because once again, someone assumed they knew what was best for me better than I did.

That Revlon money helped buy my plane ticket to visit Howard. The trip I planned entirely on my own, told no one about until it was already done. Paid my own application fee. Made my own plans.

My light had funded my own future.

And I almost talked myself out of letting her see it.

In college, I made the Washington Bullets dance team.

For those who don't know the name, the Bullets became the Washington Wizards. But back then, they were the Bullets. And I was on their dance team. I was in my element, performing, moving, doing the thing my body had always known how to do, surrounded by professional athletes at the highest level.

I sent photos home. Me in uniform, courtside with players like Michael Jordan, visiting opponents whose names people recognized everywhere, standing in spaces that felt like evidence of a life expanding.

I was proud. Genuinely, cleanly proud. The kind of proud that makes you want to share it with the people who loved you first.

And then, through the grapevine, I learned that a trusted extended family member, someone older, someone I loved, had been telling people that I thought I was better than them now.

Not: look how far she's gone.

Not: we're proud of her.

She thinks she's better than us now.

I never said a word. They were significantly older. You didn't do that. So I absorbed it. And I adjusted.

The call was coming from inside the house.

And the lesson arrived without anyone teaching it: be careful what you share. Even with people who love you. Even with people who are supposed to celebrate you. The tender things, the proud things, the dreaming things, keep those close. Keep those protected. Because joy, offered openly, can be turned into a verdict.

I didn't stop being proud of my life.

I just stopped sending it home.

Even writing this, I can feel it. Naming my own accomplishments on the page feels dangerously close to humble bragging — something I despise. But that discomfort is the rule talking. And I'm not letting it edit me this time.

The second rule:

Don't shine too brightly.

Not because I doubted my talent —

I knew I could dance. I knew I was smart. I knew I had fire.

But brightness attracts attention.

And attention had already burned me.

So I learned to dim just enough

to stay out of the line of fire.

This one I had been practicing since I was small enough to be scooped up and carried out the door.

Too much light draws attention.

And attention in an unpredictable house can go either way.

I shared a locker with my best friend in high school.

One day, the locker did what overstuffed lockers do. Everything spilled. Books, papers, the accumulated chaos of a high school life that didn't have enough space to contain it.

And among the things that hit the floor was a composition notebook. The black and white kind. The kind we used in English class for journaling.

It fell open.

And I read what was on the page. I hate CeWyon. Written over and over. Not once, not a passing thought scribbled in a bad moment. The same four words, repeated across the page like a practice drill.

Then the rest of it. The boy who liked me instead of her. The homecoming court she'd always wanted to be on and kept watching me win. The accumulated weight of everything she'd wanted that seemed to find its way to me instead.

My best friend. The girl I trusted with my locker. The girl I thought was in my corner.

I never confronted her. I just quietly stepped back. Cut the thread without explaining why. To this day she has never asked why.

That was my first heartbreak from outside my family.

It fundamentally changed how I trust girl friends.

Because here's what that notebook taught me about brightness: it doesn't just attract cruelty from strangers. It attracts it from people who smile at you every day. People who stand next to you in the hallway and laugh at your jokes and share your locker and write things they can't say to your face.

You can't always see it coming.

So you learn to dim. Not all the way. Just enough to make yourself a smaller target.

The third rule:

Stay ahead of the hurt.

If someone beat me to the punchline,

I'd make myself the joke first.

If something good happened,

I'd downplay it.

If someone complimented me,

I'd redirect it.

It wasn't humility.

It was armor.

I'd been building this armor since childhood.

In a house where good news could get swallowed by the next argument, where joy and loss shared the same evening — you learned not to let anything sit too high.

High school basketball game. I was in my cheerleader uniform.

One of my biggest offenders walked into the restroom while I was there washing my hands. Not looking in the mirror. Not admiring myself. Just washing my hands.

But I felt her walk in. Felt the energy change the way it does when someone carries resentment into a room. And before she could say anything, before she could land whatever she had loaded up to fire:

I said something self-deprecating.

Something that communicated: I know I'm not all that. Don't worry. I don't think I'm cute.

I beat her to it. Got there first. Defused the situation before it could escalate by making myself the punchline.

What I understand now is that her issue was never really about me at all. She wasn't reacting to my arrogance. She was reacting to her own envy. She thought I was cute and resented me for it. I wasn't the problem. Her feelings about me were.

I spent years managing other people's feelings about my light. Dimming myself preemptively so their envy would have nothing to grip onto. Apologizing in advance for existing in a way that made them uncomfortable.

That was never my job.

It never was.

And the fourth rule —

the one that shaped everything that came after:

Never let them see you break.

Crying, frustration, disappointment, confusion —

those had become things I only allowed myself in private.
Because in middle school,
the second you let the world see where you're tender,
somebody will press there again.
So I built a habit of walking with my head high
even when my heart was low.
Of smiling through the sting.
Of holding myself together
because falling apart felt dangerous.
This was the rule that started youngest.

In a home where I had been the adjuster, the mediator, the one who held herself together because the adults in the room required it: breaking was never an option.

Maitland confirmed it.

And the fourth rule kept me upright in every room that required it. Professional rooms. Personal ones. Rooms where I was the only one who knew how much it was costing me to stay composed.

I didn't want to seem needy.

People who know me now can barely believe the stories I tell. Because the outside was always fine. Always handled. Always together.

Whatever happens in this house stays in this house. I was that, incarnate.

And my mother didn't know I needed anything.

Because I had decided, long before she could decide for me, that I didn't.

And over time, those rules didn't feel like rules anymore.

They became rhythm. Reflex. Instinct.

Which means by the time the cost showed up, I didn't even recognize it as a cost.

I was in my early forties the first time I said it out loud.

A mother myself by then. Two daughters. Old enough to know better than to keep carrying something that heavy. Young enough to still be afraid to put it down.

My mother was visiting from Orlando. One of those ordinary Atlanta days that doesn't announce itself as anything significant. We were on the couch together, probably watching television, the way we did when the world slowed down enough to let us just be in the same room.

A talk show. Someone on the screen mentioned being a middle child. Feeling invisible.

I felt it in my chest before I felt it in my mouth.

I turned to her. Casually. On purpose.

"I was a true middle child," I said. "I always felt Todd was your favorite. Cory was Dad's. And I was the only girl, and I just… felt out of place."

She looked at me like I had said something in a language she hadn't known I spoke.

Surprised first. Then concerned.

"What makes you say that?" she said.

I chose my words carefully. She was my mother. I wasn't there to wound her.

"Remember how you and Dad were always on Todd and Cory about their homework? Checking in, asking questions, holding them accountable?" I paused. "You never asked about mine. I never understood that."

The silence that followed was not empty.

It was full of every year I had decided my needs were the ones that could wait.

And then she said it.

I didn't know you needed that.

She wasn't defending herself. She was genuinely pained. Genuinely surprised. This woman who had sacrificed her whole life for us had no idea that one of us had been quietly, carefully, competently disappearing.

Because I had made it so easy for her not to know.

The rules kept me safe.

They also made me invisible.

Even to my own mother.

By high school, I wasn't the girl in the bathroom stall anymore.

I was the girl who looked unbothered.

The girl who handled things.

The girl whose confidence appeared effortless

because she'd built it into reflex.

Not fake confidence —

just the edited version.

I was still strong.

Still talented.

Still responsible.

Still impressive.

But I was also careful.

Every move weighed.

Every truth filtered.

People saw my capability.

They didn't see my caution.

Because when you learn early that being fully yourself can hurt,

you grow into a version of yourself that's always scanning the room

before you step inside it.

You become both bold and wary.

Visible and guarded.

Strong and self-protective.
A contradiction that looks balanced from the outside
but feels exhausting on the inside.
"Play it safe."
"Don't draw too much attention."
"Don't get too excited."
"Don't take up too much space."
"Don't let anyone see all of you."
"Don't trust praise."
"Don't trust possibility."
"Don't trust being chosen."
But the most powerful one —
the rule that shaped my entire adult life —
was this:
If being yourself might lead to humiliation,
then stay small enough to avoid being seen.
And that's why the doors I was meant to walk through
felt overwhelming.
Why opportunities triggered panic.
Why compliments felt suspicious.
Why reinvention was easier than staying.
Why leaving felt safer than stepping up.
Why brilliance felt like a liability
instead of a gift.
That girl didn't disappear.
She simply shifted.
She became careful Little Me.
Edited Little Me.
Dimmed Little Me.
Survival-mode Little Me.
And she's the one we meet next.

Because if you really want to understand the woman I became,
you have to meet the girl I used to be
before the edits,
before the shrinking,
before the self-protection —
the girl I left behind on that walkway
and in that bathroom stall.
She's been waiting.

Chapter 7

The Mecca Couldn't Fix What I Brought With Me

The first time I walked into a classroom at Howard University, I almost stopped moving.

Not from nerves.

From the sound.

You couldn't actually hear a hallelujah chorus. But you could almost feel one — rising up from somewhere underneath the ordinary noise of chairs scraping and notebooks opening and people finding their seats.

Brown faces. Everywhere.

After English Estates. After Maitland. After Edgewater. After years of being the only one, or one of two, or one of a handful — here was a room full of people who looked like me.

And we were not a monolith.

We were many versions of us: different backgrounds, different stories, different parts of the country and the world. All gathered on this hallowed ground for the singular purpose of going further. Black excellence wasn't one thing at Howard. It was everything.

Brilliant people. Beautiful people. People the world had been telling me, in quiet and not-so-quiet ways, were exceptional when they existed at all.

And there I was. One of them.

I belonged here. I could feel it.

And then, almost immediately, I found a new way to feel like I didn't.

Honey, I was a mess.

Not the bad kind. The overwhelmed kind. The kind of mess that happens when something you didn't know you were starving for suddenly appears on the table in front of you and you don't quite know how to eat.

Because Howard wasn't just a university. It was the Mecca. The standard. A place where everyone seemed to arrive already extraordinary. The most beautiful. The most talented. The valedictorian. The salutatorian. The dancer. The vocalist. The legacy. The one who had already been on television, already published something, already done the thing you were just beginning to dream about.

I walked into that world and my impostor syndrome, which had made the trip without being invited, looked around and said:

Oh good. New material.

The first test came before I'd even found my rhythm.

We were going around a circle introducing ourselves. Name, where you're from, something about yourself. Simple enough. I'd done this a hundred times.

When it was my turn, I mentioned where I'd grown up. Eatonville, Florida. The oldest Black incorporated town in the country.

A fellow student across the circle nearly came out of her seat.

Her eyes went wide. Her voice caught. She pressed her hand to her chest like I'd said something sacred.

"Eatonville?" she said. "Like — Zora Neale Hurston's Eatonville from *Their Eyes Were Watching God*?"

She loved that book. Deeply, completely, the way people love things that have changed them. And here I was — from the very place that had shaped the woman who wrote it.

And I knew almost nothing about any of it.

I smiled. I nodded. I said something that wasn't a lie but wasn't the whole truth either — which was that I hadn't grown up steeped in Zora the way this woman clearly had. That my connection to Eatonville was geography, not legacy. That I had lived there without fully understanding what I was living inside.

On the outside: gracious, warm, present.

On the inside: my impostor syndrome had pulled up a chair and was taking notes.

See? Everyone here knows things you don't. Everyone here has already done the reading. You don't belong in this circle. You just got lucky with your zip code.

And yet.

There was Dr. Braxton.

Arguably one of the most challenging English professors on campus. A reputation for F's that arrived before she did. A New England accent so precise it felt like its own argument for excellence. Perfectly coiffed. Impeccably dressed. The kind of professor whose presence in a room rearranged the air.

I was afraid of her.

I was also, it turned out, made for her class.

I didn't ace her writing assignments immediately. But I routinely earned the highest scores in the class. Her praise was a grade. An A, given rarely, meant something because of how rarely it was given. Dr. Braxton did not traffic in fanfare. That came from my classmates, who marveled at how I'd earned a B when no one else had come close. I lamented the missed points nonetheless.

The first time I saw an A on my paper, I was ecstatic.

Not relieved. Not surprised in the deflecting way I usually experienced good news. Genuinely, cleanly ecstatic. I let myself feel it. I let the pride land.

Language arts was my gift. I had always known it. And here was one of the most exacting minds on campus confirming it in the only currency she dealt in.

I walked out of Dr. Braxton's class on those days feeling like myself — the real one, the unedited one, the one that knew things and wasn't afraid to show it.

And then I walked into Dr. Kwak's Calculus class.

And the floor dropped out.

Same person. Same day. Same campus. Completely different internal weather.

In Dr. Braxton's room I was a writer. In Dr. Kwak's room I was certain — certain — that I was out of my league. That everyone else had been given a manual I hadn't received. That the equation on the board was written in a language everyone around me spoke fluently and I was just nodding along, hoping nobody noticed.

That's the thing about impostor syndrome that nobody tells you.

It doesn't cover everything. It finds your gaps. The places where you can't fall back on a known gift. And it sets up camp there and makes you feel like those gaps define you more than your gifts do.

Dr. Braxton's A said: you belong here.

Dr. Kwak's chalkboard said: are you sure?

And the voice underneath both of them said: don't get too comfortable.

Then there was the dare.

I was in the dance studio warming up for Howard's dance ensemble rehearsal when I saw it. A notice posted on the wall. Washington Bullets dance team auditions.

My fellow dancer saw me looking.

"I bet you won't try out," she said.

"I bet I will," I said.

And then it escalated the way those things do between two people who are equally stubborn and equally competitive and equally unwilling to be the one who blinks.

We encouraged others. Several of us from the dance ensemble walked into those auditions together.

Five made it.

We were among them.

The auditions were enormous. Multiple rounds, multiple days, each cut announced in front of everyone who hadn't been cut yet. The dancers who intimidated me most were there — the ones who kicked to the ceiling, whose technique was flawless, whose self-assurance filled the room before they even began moving. The ones who looked like they had already been chosen.

They didn't make it.

Each time I survived a round I felt two things simultaneously, and there was no resolving them into one:

Yasss.

Say whattt.

The finals were held in a crowded mall. Public. Loud. The kind of space where nothing is private and everything echoes.

When they called our names, all five of us, we jumped up and down like we'd won the lottery.

Because we had.

That joy was real. Unguarded, unedited, full-bodied joy. The kind I didn't always let myself feel. It landed completely. This was going to be fun.

And then came the first rehearsal.

The team voted.

Not coaches. Not administrators. The women who had watched me audition, who had jumped up and down with me in that mall, who knew exactly what they were choosing.

Captain.

And just like that — the joy left the building.

Not dramatically. Not all at once. Just quietly, quickly, replaced by something familiar.

Uh-oh.

I had felt this before. The freeze that arrives not when something goes wrong but when something goes right in a way that requires something of you. When the fun becomes responsibility. When the dare becomes a title.

I had felt it when they called my name at Miss Black Orlando — the pageant I had been circling my entire childhood, performing in it for years before I was old enough to compete, admiring the big girls from the stage, waiting my turn with the patience of someone who knows her moment is coming but doesn't quite believe it yet. When I finally won, I felt it then too.

Numbness. Then the machinery of composure.

Something in me had learned so early not to trust being chosen for anything serious that when it finally arrived, my body flinched instead of receiving it.

So instead of sitting in the captaincy, I went straight to calculation.

Because being captain meant something I hadn't fully considered when I said I bet I will in that studio.

I would get to choose the music.

I would get to choreograph.

Suddenly the terror of not feeling good enough had a counterweight — a creative hunger that was worth every bit of the fear. The stage I didn't want living with me had handed me something I actually wanted.

A reason to stay.

I stood in that role: leading, creating, performing at a professional level. Some part of me was still waiting for someone to tap me on the shoulder and say, "We meant to pick someone else."

It doesn't excuse you just because you've earned something. It just moves the goalpost. You make the team and it says: but can you lead? You lead and it says: but do you really belong? You belong and it says: but for how long?

Howard gave me so much. Community. Excellence reflected back at me in every direction. A classroom where I finally felt racially at home. A professor who demanded my best and got it. A dare that became a captaincy I didn't believe I deserved.

The Mecca couldn't fix what I brought with me. Neither could I. Not yet.

Chapter 8

Running From My Own Light Like I Owed It Money

By the time I traced my patterns back to that walkway, that bathroom stall, and that night with the letter, I had to admit something hard.

I did not just learn to survive.

I learned to run.

And not a casual jog, either.

I am talking full-sprint, arms-pumping, don't-look-back, somebody-call-a-coach running.

If avoidance were an Olympic sport, I would not just have medals.

I would have a signature shoe.

A documentary.

Probably a limited-edition Wheaties box with my face on it and a slogan that said: Not enough. Not yet.

Every time life tried to hand me the microphone labeled "Your Voice," I suddenly had somewhere else to be.

An errand, a different job, a perfectly reasonable reinvention.

Another polished goodbye with panic just beneath the surface.

People have always assumed the spotlight fits me.

They see the way I walk into a room, the way I connect with people, the way strangers turn into friends in ten seconds flat, and they think I must love every bit of it.

I don't.

I can handle a room. I know how to show up. I know how to hold space and hold attention and make people feel like the most important person I've talked to all week.

But I don't draw energy from being on all the time.

I'm a social introvert who knows how to be warm and present, but I need quiet to breathe afterward.

I don't love the stage.

I simply don't fear it.

If you hand me a microphone, I will meet the moment.

But that doesn't mean I want the moment living with me.

The issue has never been visibility.

It has always been being heard.

Looking sharp is easy.

Performing is natural.

Leading feels like breathing.

But talking from my soul: the real stuff, the true stuff, the stuff that takes something to say. That used to stop me cold.

Every aptitude test, every personality quiz, every career assessment I ever took pointed me toward the same calling.

Leader.

Communicator.

Speaker.

Coach.

Teacher.

Voice.

All roles that require presence, truth, and the willingness to be actually known.

You think I listened?

Absolutely not.

I treated those results like spam mail.

Return to sender. Wrong girl.

I wasn't confused.

I was avoiding something I had learned very young.

My voice could get me in trouble.

I started talking early.

Too early, if you asked the grown-ups who swore I entered the world mid-conversation.

My voice was tiny and high-pitched, always chirping and questioning, always reaching for the next thing to understand.

My dad called me Chick because I never stopped making noise.

I loved to learn.

Loved it so much that when I read my first sight word, I nearly threw myself a parade.

Books felt like treasure.

Questions felt like oxygen.

I was the child who asked why after every answer, not to be difficult, but because the world genuinely fascinated me and I couldn't imagine pretending otherwise.

And grown-ups loved that about me.

Until they didn't.

Until my questions stopped being cute and started being accurate.

Until my honesty started revealing things people preferred stayed hidden.

Until my curiosity hit nerves nobody wanted touched.

And underneath all of that —
underneath the chirping and the questions and the parades for sight words —
there were things happening to me.
Quiet things.
Secret things.
Paid for with handfuls of candy corn and a whispered promise not to tell.

.

.

.

I didn't have words for it then.
I choose not to give it many now.
I sat with that for a long time before I understood its full impact on me.
But I want you to know it happened.
And I want you to know what it taught me, because that's the part that followed me out of that room and into every room after it:
That my body was not entirely mine.
That my truth could be purchased.
That silence could be required of me before I was old enough to understand what silence cost.
I didn't break.
Children rarely do, at least not in ways the world can see.
I just kept going.
The way children do.
The way they have to.
But something reorganized itself inside me in that quiet, the way furniture shifts after an earthquake: everything still standing, nothing quite in the same place.

I didn't grow quiet.

I grew careful.

Not small, just edited.

Not obedient, just aware of the cost of honesty.

Not shy, just learning, faster than any child should have to, which parts of myself were safe to show and which parts needed guarding.

I was headstrong until the punishments made me hesitant.

Curious until the consequences taught me caution.

A truth-teller until the truth revealed too much.

I didn't lose my fire.

I learned to hide it.

And once you learn to hide your fire young, the hiding becomes fluent.

Automatic.

You don't even notice you're doing it anymore.

You just know, the way you know to look both ways before crossing a street, that some things are kept inside and some things are not.

And your voice —

your real voice, the one that demands something to use —

falls into the category of things you protect.

I chose roles where I could shine without ever revealing anything real.

I could lead without being vulnerable.

I could show up without uncovering my truth.

I could be on without being open.

I could be impressive without being known.

People thought I was walking in my purpose.

Meanwhile, I was strategically avoiding the one thing my purpose required.

My voice.

Purpose would tap my shoulder and I would sidestep it like I hadn't felt a thing.

That wasn't me. I wasn't even here.

But purpose is patient.

Purpose circles the block.

It doesn't forget.

Every opportunity I turned down.

Every test result I dismissed.

Every room I walked out of before it could ask something real of me.

And every time I declined, I told myself a story: Not yet. Not me. Not this.

But the truth, the one I was not ready to say out loud, was simpler and harder than any of those.

I wasn't lost.

I wasn't unqualified.

I wasn't confused about my direction.

I was hiding.

Because stepping into my calling required the one thing I had learned, in the quietest and most consequential way, to protect.

My truth.

My fire, unhidden.

And there came a day, not dramatic, not cinematic, just quiet and unmistakable, when I realized I was strong enough to carry the heat of my own light.

Not because the old lessons had disappeared.

But because I understood where they came from.

The running had a price I didn't tally until much later.

Not just the rooms I entered sideways and the doors I closed before they fully opened.

The price was the version of me that existed in the gap between who I actually was and who I was willing to let the world see.

That gap is exhausting to maintain. You have to be vigilant every moment. You have to know which version of yourself is appropriate for which room. You have to track what you've revealed and what you've protected and who knows what and whether any of it is consistent.

It is a full-time job. Unpaid. With no benefits. And no days off.

The running kept me safe. I understand that now. Every exit was a form of protection. Every reinvention was my body choosing the path of least threat. I wasn't weak. I was wired. There is a difference.

But the wiring that kept me safe at seven was taking something significant from me at forty-seven.

The question stopped being: how do I keep myself safe?

And became: what am I still running from?

The answer, when I finally sat still long enough to hear it, was nothing.

Nothing real. Nothing present. Nothing that existed in the room I was actually standing in.

I was running from ghosts. Old ones. Ones that had stopped having any power over me the moment I understood where they came from.

That's where the running stopped.

Not all at once.

Not without looking back.

But stopped.

And I turned around.

Chapter 9

The Gift My Body Chose
Before I Could

You already know about the Saturday mornings. The music.
The album on repeat. The way my mother pressed play and
we all moved through the house like the night before hadn't
happened.

But my body wasn't just responding to my mother's ritual.
It was doing something on its own. Something it had already
learned to do before anyone handed it a song or a rhythm or a
reason.

My body knew how to find its way back before my mind had
any language for what it was coming back from.

My body was already writing rules I would follow for decades.

Stay bright, but not too bright.

Show up, but don't reveal too much.

Succeed, but don't believe it.

Shine, but stay guarded.

Be impressive, but never assume you belong.

On the outside, I looked like someone who moved through life with ease. New job? I rose. New challenge? I rose. New space? I adapted, excelled, impressed, delivered.

On the inside, I was still operating under the same rules my body had learned in that living room — the rules written in me long before I understood what trauma or regulation or coping mechanisms were.

But here's the part that still amazes me.

Long before I had words for pain, my body had already found its own way to carry it.

It found music.

Not in a recital hall or a dance studio.

In the living room.

On the mornings after.

And it used dance to translate what I couldn't say.

And the surprising part?

I didn't even find dance.

Dance found me.

One day in third grade, a woman stopped me and said she'd been watching me walk.

"Your movement is so graceful," she said.

"Have you ever thought about dancing?"

I hadn't.

I didn't think of myself as anything special.

But she saw something I didn't.

She invited me to join her team.

And I said yes, without understanding I'd just stepped into the one thing that would hold me together during some of the hardest years of my life.

People assumed I loved dance.

But that was never quite true.

I loved music.

Music rearranged the air inside my body.

Music gave me something to cling to when everything else felt unpredictable, a steady pulse I could hold onto when the rest of the world kept shifting under my feet.

Music could shift my mood faster than any conversation ever could.

Dance was just what happened to me when the music hit.

Dance wasn't my passion.

It was my translation.

My body's way of saying what I was too afraid to speak.

And yes, people complimented me.

They told me I was good, talented, captivating even.

And I smiled, nodded, said thank you —

but inside I felt confused.

Great dancer?

Me?

I didn't feel great.

I felt grateful.

Grateful for a place where the rules were different.

Where I didn't have to be careful.

Where no one mocked the way I moved.

Where I didn't have to second-guess my excitement.

Where my body could tell the truth I had learned to hide.

Years later, when I learned about trauma responses, childhood adversity, the patterns that stuck, and how the body stores what the mind can't handle, everything clicked into place.

Dance regulated what my childhood dysregulated.

Movement metabolized what I suppressed.

Music soothed what my environment stirred up.

Rhythm held what I couldn't yet say.

Dance may not have been my calling,
but it absolutely was my rescue.
And now I can see it clearly:
Every time trauma tried to silence me,
my body put me in motion.
Every time my voice froze,
my body found rhythm.
Every time life dimmed me,
my body found light.
And layered beneath all of that was a truth I didn't understand
until much later:
Opportunities always had a way of finding me.
Even the ones I didn't ask for.
Even the ones I didn't feel ready for.
Even the ones I tried to hide from.
Leadership found me.
Dance found me.
Music found me.
Purpose wasn't done with me.
And eventually, understanding found me too.
Because the day I learned about impostor syndrome —
what it was, what it meant, how it worked —
was the first time in my entire life that something felt like
relief.
Not confusion.
Not judgment.
Not shame.
Relief.
"Oh…
this is a thing?
There's a name for this?

This isn't because I'm broken?"
It lifted a weight I didn't know I'd been carrying.
A heaviness I thought was personality.
A burden I assumed was my fault.
A tension I had mistaken for "just how I am."
And once that weight shifted,
everything around it moved too.
What came next —
the research, the psychology, the science, the somatic truth,
the childhood connections —
began rearranging the way I saw myself.
That moment is where my real healing began.
I still use it.
Not as performance.
Not as exercise.
As medicine.
Years later, moving through perimenopause, body unsettled,
mood unpredictable, everything inside me doing things I hadn't
asked it to do, I found myself reaching for the same thing I had
reached for at eight years old.
Not a prescription.
Not a protocol.
A song.
I found adult dance classes.
Soul line dancing.
Or I would simply put on Daft Punk's "Lose Yourself to Dance"
— Pharrell's voice, that groove that doesn't ask permission — in
the middle of the afternoon
and let my body do what it already knew how to do.
The happy chemicals arrive before the first verse is over.
Every time.

The body doesn't forget what regulates it.

Even when the mind has spent decades trying to think its way to calm,

the body already knows the shortcut.

It learned it on a stranger's floor.

It refined it in a dance studio at eight years old.

And it still works.

Fifty years later.

That's not a coincidence.

That's the body retaining what it learned, the good and the hard, long after the moment has passed.

I think about that a lot. The way the body holds onto what healed it just as tenaciously as it holds onto what hurt it. We talk so much about trauma storage, the way old wounds stay lodged in tissue and tension and reflex. But the body keeps the good things too. The things that regulated it. The things that gave it relief when everything else felt unmanageable.

Music was always mine. Long before I understood what it was doing, my body understood. Long before I had a name for what it meant to feel steadier again, my body had already found its own version of it in a melody, a rhythm, a song that rearranged the air inside me and made the next hour possible.

That's not a small thing. That's a gift. The kind you don't recognize as a gift until you're old enough to look back and understand what it was carrying you through.

My body knew before I did.

It usually does.

Chapter 10

Oh. There's a Name For This.

I didn't meet impostor syndrome in a therapist's office.
Or during a deep, reflective moment.
Or sitting still with a cup of tea, ready for personal growth.
No.
I met it the way I meet most life-changing things —
while multitasking, scrolling, half-distracted, and minding my business.

I came across an article by Dr. Valerie Young,
and the story she opened with made me stop mid-scroll.

It was about graduate women in academia, women who had already earned their credentials, already built their careers, already proved themselves in their fields, gathered at a symposium.

These were not beginners.
Not students finding their footing.
Women who had done the work, published the papers, sat at the tables, held the titles.
And yet, when they were asked how they felt in those rooms, so many of them admitted:
"I don't think I belong here."

"Admissions must have made a mistake."

"Everyone here is smarter."

"I'm just waiting for them to figure out I shouldn't be in this program."

I read that and literally blinked at the screen.

"THEM?

They feel like THAT too?"

And that realization brought a relief I felt in my body first —

a loosening in my chest I didn't even know was tight.

Because for the first time, I thought:

"Maybe nothing is wrong with me."

And once that landed?

Oh, baby.

I did not sit still with that revelation.

I went into a full-blown CeWyon-style research spiral.

I didn't breathe, journal, reflect, or sip water.

No gently easing into awareness.

I went into investigative reporting mode

like somebody had assigned me a dissertation with a midnight deadline.

Tabs. Everywhere.

Articles. Studies. Diagrams. Psychology papers. Interviews. Blogs. Charts.

PDFs I absolutely did not need.

I had so many browser windows open, my laptop started making that "please stop" sound.

I wasn't reading casually.

I was studying.

Every sentence felt like a clue.

Every paragraph felt personal.

Every bullet point felt like somebody had followed me since childhood with a clipboard.

And the deeper I went, the more my internal commentary escalated.

"Wait… this is me."

"Oh, this is DEFINITELY me."

"Hold on, are they reading my diary?"

"I need to call someone…

Actually, no I don't. Let me keep reading."

I wasn't just connecting dots.

I was drawing constellations.

Because suddenly it all made sense:

The running. The shrinking. The perfectionism. The leaving before I felt exposed. The fear underneath praise. The panic behind opportunity. The hiding inside competence. The second-guessing. The overachieving. The carefulness.

Not as flaws.

Not as lack of confidence.

Not as spiritual weakness.

Not as personality.

As adaptation.

As protection.

As instinct —protecting me before I even understood what I was protecting myself from.

And then the research took me somewhere I hadn't expected.

I wasn't just reading about impostor syndrome anymore. I was reading about what lives underneath it. About childhood adversity. About ACEs, Adverse Childhood Experiences, a term I had never encountered before that night, sitting there in the dark with my laptop screen as the only light in the room.

And I went still.

Because suddenly there was a name for it. Not just for the impostor syndrome. For the thing that had grown it. The environment that had installed it. The childhood that had written the code.

From there it kept going. Trauma responses. Attachment wounds. The back-and-forth between feeling and thought.

Not as a list. As a trail. Each one leading to the next, each one landing somewhere personal.

From there the trail led to cognitive bias. Confirmation bias specifically — the way the brain seeks out evidence that confirms what it already believes and filters out anything that contradicts it.

Which meant: if I believed, somewhere deep and unexamined, that I wasn't quite enough, that I was one mistake away from being exposed, that the praise was generous but the reality was provisional, then my brain had been helpfully collecting evidence for that belief for decades. Curating it. Filing it carefully. Presenting it to me at inconvenient moments as proof.

My brain had been building a case against me.

Using my own memories as evidence. My own experiences as exhibit A. My own history as the prosecution's star witness.

And I'd been sitting in the defendant's chair so long I had forgotten I was allowed to object.

Another tab. Early childhood experiences and the formation of core beliefs. The idea that what we experience before the age of seven, before the prefrontal cortex is fully developed, before we have the cognitive tools to contextualize or question, becomes the operating system. Not a file. Not a folder. The actual operating system, running in the background of everything that comes after.

I thought about four-year-old me walking out of kindergarten.

I thought about roll call.

I thought about the pallet.

All of it happening before I had the tools to understand any of it. All of it being absorbed and filed and incorporated into the operating system of a child who had no idea she was being shaped.

She was just living. She was just surviving. She was just doing what children do, which is absorb everything in their environment and make meaning from it as best they can.

And the meaning she made, the only meaning available to a child with limited context and limited language and unlimited sensitivity, was:

Something must be wrong with me.

Not because it was true.

Because it was early.

And early, in the architecture of a human mind, carries a weight that late understanding has to work very hard to lift.

Two books found me. Not at the same time. At separate points along the road.

The first was Dr. Bessel van der Kolk's *The Body Keeps the Score: Brain, Mind, and Body in the Healing of Trauma.*

I cannot tell you how many times I had to put that book down

just to stare at the wall.

Not because it was difficult.

Because it was accurate.

Van der Kolk writes about how trauma lives in the body —

not just in the memory, not just in the mind,

but in the tissue, the gut,

the way your shoulders rise before you even know you're afraid.

I thought about my jaw.

The one I'd been unclenching my whole life
without ever asking why it was clenched.
I thought about the way I scanned rooms.
The way my body went on alert before my brain caught up.
The way certain words — *cute* being one of them —
could reach all the way back to a hallway at Maitland Junior
High
without my permission.
The body had been carrying all of it the entire time.
I just hadn't known how to read what it was holding.
Then, at a different point entirely, the second book appeared:
*What Happened to You? Conversations on Trauma, Resilience,
and Healing*
by Oprah Winfrey and Dr. Bruce D. Perry.
Its entire premise is a shift from asking
What's wrong with you?
to asking
What happened to you?
I had already made that shift.
Alone, at a computer screen, reading about ACEs
long before I knew that question had a name,
had science behind it,
had been explored by one of the world's leading trauma experts
in conversation with one of the most influential women alive.
Finding that book wasn't a lesson.
It was a confirmation.

Understanding something intellectually and feeling it
in your body are two different countries. You can know a
thing completely, be able to explain it to someone else with
perfect clarity, cite the research, trace the patterns, name the

mechanisms, and still wake up the next morning with the same old weight in the same old places.

The mind learns fast. The body learns slow.

The first thing I noticed wasn't emotional.

It was physical.

My breath deepened before my thoughts did.

My shoulders dropped somewhere I hadn't realized they'd been living —

up near my ears, apparently, for most of my adult life.

And then, quietly, almost shyly:

"I'm not crazy."

That was the first real thought.

Not "I'm healed."

Not "I have all the answers now."

Just —

I'm not crazy.

And if you've spent decades quietly wondering whether your reactions were too much, your fears were irrational, your self-doubt was a personal failing —

you know exactly how much those three words weigh.

They weigh everything.

My therapist was the first to point out what the body was still doing. We were in a session, and I was talking about the physical violations I had experienced as a child. At some point she stopped me and asked whether I had noticed that my fists were clenched as I spoke.

I hadn't noticed.

Not once. Not ever. My body had been responding to the memory the same way it had responded to the original experience, tightening, going on alert, and I had no idea. It was so familiar it had become invisible. That was just how I held myself. That was just Tuesday.

The real landing came later. At a personal growth retreat, in a room full of people I mostly didn't know. Some familiar faces from other retreats, no one I was close to. All of us there with the same purpose: to do the kind of work that doesn't happen at a desk.

We took turns in the seat.

When it was your turn, you sat in the chair at the front of the room and shared what you most wished someone had said to you. The thing you had needed to hear and hadn't. The words that might have changed something if they'd arrived earlier, from the right mouth, in the right room.

Mine was simple.

You are enough.

Not you are smart. Not you are capable. Not you belong here. I'd been making cases for all of those my entire life. Just this.

As you are. Without the credentials. Without the competence. Without the careful management of how much of yourself you let the room see.

Enough.

Then the room turned toward me.

One by one, and then together, they said it. The facilitator varied the volume, the pitch, the pace. First a whisper, then building, the words arriving in waves from people who had no history with me, no obligation to mean it, no reason to say it except that they were in a room together choosing to offer what they themselves still needed to receive.

Strangers, mostly. People who didn't know my name before that weekend.

And something in my body heard it differently than my mind ever had.

At the height of it, the room full of voices, the words landing from every direction, I felt it.

Not as a thought. Not as emotion.

As sensation.

In my left shoulder.

The place where I had apparently been storing things I didn't know I was storing. The weight of rooms I'd walked into braced. The tension of words I'd swallowed. The weight of decades of careful, calibrated, everything-is-fine.

I felt it there, concentrated and undeniable.

And then, as I breathed, as I let the words in rather than deflecting them with gratitude and a quick subject change, I felt it begin to subside.

Not gone. Not instantly resolved.

But loosening.

The way something loosens when it finally gets permission to.

Van der Kolk was right. The body had been keeping score the entire time. Not in a journal. Not in a memory I could examine and set aside. In my left shoulder. In my jaw. In the particular way I held myself in rooms that required something of me.

And in that chair, with those voices, some of it began to let go.

You are enough.

I had read those words. Written them. Said them to other people with complete conviction.

That day was the first time my body believed them.

So I sought therapy.

Specifically, EMDR:

Eye Movement Desensitization and Reprocessing, a body-based therapy that works directly with the places where trauma settles rather than relying on talk alone. It was a game-changer for the childhood experiences that had taken up permanent residence inside me long before I'd even recognized that what I was carrying was anything other than normal.

The Big T traumas —

the ones that happened to my body before my mind could protect me —

those required a trained clinician.

A professional.

Someone who knew how to help a body

put down what it had been carrying

since before I was old enough to understand the weight.

I say this not as a disclaimer.

I say it as an act of love toward anyone reading this

who is carrying something similar.

A book can change your life.

A framework can transform your thinking.

Awareness is the beginning of everything.

But some wounds need more than awareness.

Some wounds need a witness.

A trained one.

And there is no weakness in knowing the difference.

There is only wisdom.

Some people say impostor syndrome isn't real.

I understand the argument.

The term is catchy, but it flattens something much deeper.

It makes it sound like millions of people just independently decided

to feel fraudulent,

when in reality, many of us were trained into it

long before adulthood.

So call it impostor syndrome.

Call it impostor phenomenon.
Call it conditioned self-doubt, survival wiring,
or the quiet fear of being exposed as not enough.
The label isn't the point.
The point is that people are living with it.
And their bodies, choices, careers, and confidence
are paying the toll.
We don't get free by arguing terminology.
We get free by telling the truth about what shaped us.

And here's what nobody tells you about the day you stop
believing you are the problem:
It's not loud.
There's no announcement.
No confetti.
No version of you standing in a field with the wind in your
hair finally free.
It's just a Tuesday.
Or a Wednesday.
Some ordinary day when a familiar thought tries to move in
and you look at it clearly for the first time
and say —
No.
That one isn't mine.
And mean it.
And when you can finally separate your identity from your injury,
healing stops being a mystery
and starts being a possibility.

Chapter 11

Old Patterns in New Rooms

Let me tell you about the spa.

Not the finished version, the gleaming, humming, fully built-out space it became.

The before version.

The shell.

I'd been looking for a space for my new business. The franchise I'd partnered with, Hand & Stone Massage and Facial Spa, recommended 2,400 square feet, a manageable size for a first location, enough room to operate without drowning in overhead.

But I had already seen where I wanted to be.

A shopping center still under development in the heart of North Decatur: bustling, established, anchored by a Whole Foods, sitting across from a major hospital. The kind of location that tells a customer something before they even walk through your door. Half the spaces were built. Others still in process. And I knew, in the way you sometimes just know things, that this was the right ecosystem for what I was building.

The problem: every space was taken.

So I did what the woman I was becoming does.

I downloaded the schematic of the entire shopping center.

Printed it out.

And put it on my vision board.

Not a specific unit. Not a particular square footage.

The whole plaza.

The location. The energy. The foot traffic. The address.

I claimed it before I had any idea which door would open.

Then I called my broker and said, calmly, like a woman who had no reason to believe this was anything but a long shot, to reach out to the developers. Let them know I was interested. If anything fell through, I wanted to know.

Less than 24 hours later, my broker called.

A dental chain had signed the lease on one of the spaces.

And then backed out.

The space was mine if I wanted it.

I was thrilled.

Until I heard the square footage.

3,600 square feet.

Not the 2,400 the franchise recommended.

Fifteen hundred extra square feet: more than I had planned for, more than I had asked for, more than I thought I was ready for.

And the rent to match.

And right on cue, right on schedule, exactly on time —
the old voice showed up.

Who do you think you are?

Starting out this big? With this kind of overhead?

What if you're not ready?

What if you fail?

Awareness is beautiful — until life gives you a chance to use it.

Because knowing your patterns is one thing. Catching yourself while you're doing them? That's the graduate level.

I knew that voice.

I'd been hearing it my whole life, in every room that required more of me than I felt prepared to give.

I also knew where it came from.

I had done the work.

I had learned how old fear can show up in new moments.

I had read Dr. Valerie Young's work on the impostor phenomenon: that handbook that stopped me mid-scroll and made me think, *wait, she's describing me.*

I had read Dr. Susan Jeffers, who taught me that the fear doesn't go away.

You feel it and you move anyway.

I had traced my patterns back to the walkway, the bathroom stall, the candy corn, the rules I absorbed before I understood any of it.

I knew exactly why it was so loud.

I knew exactly what it was protecting.

So I refuted it.

Business 101: bring in more than you're spending.

The space was larger, yes. The rent was higher, yes.

But the capacity was also larger. The revenue potential was larger. The vision I had carried, schematic on the vision board, faith already placed. That was larger too.

My husband sat with me in that moment the way the right person does —

not telling me what to decide,

but reminding me of who I was when I couldn't quite remember.

Smart, capable.

Someone who had walked herself out of a kindergarten classroom at four years old because she knew her worth.

Someone who had survived things that would have broken most people.

Someone who had been told her whole life, in ways loud and quiet, named and unnamed, that she was too much,

and had finally, finally started to believe that too much

was exactly enough.

So before I picked up that pen —

while the old voice was still running its commentary in the background —

I negotiated.

More buildout money from the developer than my franchise had seen before.

More time rent-free than anyone expected to get.

Terrilluminated — terrified and illuminated — the entire time.

Afraid of the size of the thing and lit up by it in equal measure,

fear and fire occupying the same body,

neither one winning,

both of them real —

and still asking for more anyway.

Dr. Susan Jeffers was right.

The fear doesn't go away.

You feel it and you move anyway.

Then, and only then, I picked up the pen.

My hand shook.

I am not being dramatic: my hand genuinely shook.

So I did the only thing that made sense.

I used my other hand to steady it.

And I signed.

The woman who negotiated a record and then needed both hands to sign her name is not a contradiction.

She's just honest.

And honest is exactly what I want to be.

The space was an empty shell when I got it.

Nothing built inside yet.

Just a dirt floor and the blueprint of something that didn't exist yet.

That was seven years ago.

The spa opened. It filled. Hand & Stone Decatur became the thing I had seen on the vision board before there was any evidence it could exist.

Then a pandemic arrived and shut down every high-touch business in the country.

Mine included.

I watched businesses around me close permanently. Spas, salons, studios — places built on proximity, on hands, on trust — shuttered one after another. The math didn't work. The fear was rational. The industry I had signed into with shaking hands was being dismantled by something no one had planned for.

I stayed open.

Not easily. Not without cost. Not without months that tested every negotiation skill I had used to secure that lease in the first place.

But the woman who had steadied her own hand to sign her name was not the woman who was going to let a circumstance, even a global one, make her decision for her.

The economy still tests it. Some months still test me. This is not a story that ends with a bow on top and a revenue number that makes people clap.

This is a story about a woman who claimed a space before she felt ready, filled it with something real, survived what no one saw coming, and is still standing in it.

Seven years later.
Both hands.
Still going.
The woman who signed that lease wasn't the completed
version of herself.
She was the version brave enough to claim the space
before she felt ready to fill it.
That shaking hand, that steadying hand, that terrilluminated
moment,
the negotiation that happened before the pen ever moved —
Not loud.
Not clean.
Not without fear.
Just —
chosen.
On purpose.
With both hands.
And then some.

Chapter 12

The First Time I Spoke Without Fear of Being Judged

I need to be honest about something before this chapter earns its title.

The first time I spoke without fear of being judged, I wasn't speaking for myself.

I was speaking for the young people who weren't in the room.

That distinction matters. Because for a long time I confused the two. I thought having a voice meant being willing to use it on your own behalf, standing up for yourself, claiming your place, announcing your worth. And I couldn't do any of those things without the old calculations running in the background.

But speaking for someone else? That I could do.

The meeting was a strategic planning session. My boss, his boss, and a community stakeholder. Three exceptionally intelligent people with the gift for language and the credibility to match. I was the one who would develop and execute whatever they decided. I was the tactician. They were the architects.

And they were adding layers to the programming that would not work for the young entrepreneurs we were serving.

Not because their ideas were bad. Because they didn't know our audience. They were planning for a version of these young people that existed in their imagination, capable, yes, but also compliant, patient, willing to sit through the kind of structured process that serves institutions more than it serves kids.

I'd been in the room with these young people. I knew what lit them up and what lost them. I knew where the energy went and where it died.

And I said so.

Not loudly. Not combatively. But clearly. With the specificity of someone who had actually done the work they were planning around a conference table.

I used the word *concretize*.

To make something concrete. To give abstract ideas tangible, actionable form. The exact right word for what I was describing.

The community stakeholder barely contained her smirk.

The boss's boss said: *It's okay, we know what you meant.*

As if I had reached for something above my station and missed.

I hadn't missed.

Concretize is a word. It was the correct word. I had used it in its proper context without hesitation because that is simply how I speak when I know what I'm talking about.

I told my boss afterward because we worked in tandem and he deserved to know. I did not send anyone a screenshot of the dictionary entry, though it took everything in me not to.

I was correct.

I knew it.

That was enough.

And that, that moment of knowing something and staying with what I knew regardless of the smirk, regardless of the patronizing reassurance, regardless of the collective bless-her-heart energy in that room, was the beginning of something.

Not confidence as performance. Not the edited, calculated boldness I'd been passing off as voice for years.

Something quieter and more durable.

The knowledge that what I knew was real whether they recognized it or not.

I pushed back on their plan that day because the young people we were serving deserved a program designed by someone who actually knew them. My discomfort in that room mattered less than their experience in the one we were building for them.

I found my voice for others before I found it for myself.

That's not a failure. That's a pattern worth understanding.

I'd been doing it my whole life. Fierce about my mother. Fierce about the foster youth who needed someone to show them how close they already were. Fierce about anyone who needed someone to say the true thing in a room full of people who hadn't done the work.

For myself? Still calculating. Still editing. Still waiting to be found out.

People who know me would never call me a shrinking violet. I wasn't afraid. I wasn't passive. I just didn't think it was worth it.

I now understand I didn't think I was worth it.

That makes my heart ache for that person.

The healing closed that gap.

Not all at once. But slowly, the voice I'd used for everyone else started showing up when it was my turn too.

And when it did, it sounded exactly the same.

Clear. Unpadded. Correct.

Unafraid of what came after.

Because I'd been practicing for years.

Just not on myself.

Let me tell you about the people who saw me.

Not all of them.

Not even most of them.

But the ones who mattered —

the ones whose seeing shaped something,

even when the shaping happened sideways,

even when the gift arrived in the wrong container,

even when I wasn't yet ready to receive it.

I came to Mrs. Griffin's class after the school year had already started.

New school. Third grade. Behind before I'd begun.

She placement tested me.

And then she told me something no adult had ever said to me directly before.

Not my parents, not my teachers, not the neighbors who admired our family from the outside while the inside burned.

She said:

You are smart.

Not as encouragement.

Not as a consolation.

As a fact.

My scores, she said, were off the charts.

I remember the feeling of those words more than the words themselves —

the way they landed somewhere deep and unfamiliar,

in a place that didn't quite know what to do with being seen that clearly.

She recommended me for the gifted program.

Children like me, children whose scores said *more, further, higher*, got bussed to another school on certain days for enrichment.

I would have stayed in her classroom for everything else.

I would have just also gotten on that bus.

But the program required a family interview.

And the intake person looked at my father

and decided our home wouldn't provide the support required.

Not my scores.

Not my potential.

Not what Mrs. Griffin had seen in me and staked her recommendation on.

My father's interview.

I never got on the bus.

I'm not going to say more about that than this:

I tested off the charts

and was never once treated like it by the institutions that were supposed to confirm what the charts said.

I learned shortly after why.

The reason, it turned out, was a single word.

An expletive my father used in the intake interview.

Not a pattern. Not a red flag. Not evidence of an unsupportive home.

One word.

Hell.

And a program designed to nurture gifted children decided that was enough information to close the folder.

We were mortified.

Old enough to understand what had happened.

Young enough to have nowhere to put it.

And here is the complicated truth I need to tell you about my father:

because this book has been honest about who he was as a
husband,
and it owes you honesty about who he was as a father too:
He was plugged in.
Present.
Supportive in the ways his own broken upbringing taught
him how to be.
As terrible as he was in his marriage,
he showed up for his children.
The intake person didn't see that.
They heard one word and made their decision.
And a little girl who tested off the charts
never got on the bus.
Make of that what you will.
What I will tell you is what that bus did to me.
Every morning it came.
Every morning it left.
Without me.
And every morning it delivered the same quiet verdict:
Not quite.
Not enough.
Not this one.
Not once.
Not as a single event I could process and move past.
Every day. Reliably.
The way only routine things can wound you —
not with the shock of a single blow
but with the accumulation of a thousand small confirmations
that the conclusion you've drawn about yourself
is correct.
I wasn't being irrational.

I was being logical.
The institution had looked at my scores,
looked at my family,
and rendered a verdict.
And then sent a bus every day to remind me of it.
So when Mrs. Griffin told me I was smart —
when the difficult English teacher demanded more of me —
when anyone offered belief or permission or recognition —
it had to compete with the sound of that bus engine pulling
away.
And for a long time,
the bus was louder.
That's not a failure of confidence.
That's a child making sense of the information she was given.
The bus was wrong about me.
It just took thirty years
and a graduate classroom
and a woman ready to hear something different
to be able to say that
and mean it.
Mrs. Griffin kept me.
I don't know exactly how or why —
whether it was her choice or circumstance or both —
but I spent third grade in her classroom
and then fourth grade too.
Two years.
Two years of being seen by the person who saw me first.
She was everything.
The way she carried herself.
The standard she held.
The way she moved through a room like a woman who knew
exactly who she was and had made peace with every part of it.

I wanted to be her.

Not like her.

Her.

Eight years old and I already understood, in the wordless way children understand things, that this woman had something I wanted.

Not her job.

Not her classroom.

The way she existed inside herself.

She was the first mirror that showed me what a woman who shines looks like.

And even though I couldn't yet receive the fullness of what she was offering —

even though the system had already told me my brilliance had conditions

something in me filed it away.

That. Whatever that is. Remember that.

Years later, in middle school, a notoriously difficult English teacher pulled me aside.

Or rather: called me out.

In front of the class.

About being late.

I was the only other brown face in the room.

She was harsh. Direct. Unsparing.

She said I was squandering my brilliance by showing up to her class late.

She didn't ask why I was late.

I was taking the long way to avoid certain students in the hallway —

the same walkway, different days,

the same cruelty in different configurations.

I was managing.

She didn't know that.

She just knew I was late.

And that whatever she saw in me was not being honored by my tardiness.

I didn't receive it as care.

I received it as shame.

Which is what it felt like.

Which is perhaps what it was.

And yet —

years later, I found myself in her husband's class.

And he mentioned, almost in passing,

that his wife had talked about me before he'd ever met me.

She had taken me home with her.

In her mind. In her concern. In whatever it is that makes a hard brilliant woman keep thinking about a particular student long after the bell rings.

She never told me she believed in me.

She expressed it as demand.

As disappointment in what I wasn't yet doing with what I had.

It arrived years late.

Through the wrong messenger.

In the wrong tone.

And I had to decide whether to receive it anyway.

I did.

Eventually.

But that's the thing about seeds planted in unready soil.

They don't always know they've been planted.

They just wait.

By the time I sat down in a graduate level classroom, something had shifted.

Not loudly. Not all at once.

But the soil was different.

And I remember sitting in that classroom,

looking around at the other students,

and having a thought so simple it almost embarrassed me:

CeWyon.

You understand this material just as well as anyone in here.

Maybe better.

Stop hesitating.

Stop deferring.

Stop defaulting to uncertainty you don't actually feel.

My instructor, the hardest and most brilliant I had ever encountered, had already said so.

She noticed me.

Not the performance of me.

Not the careful, calibrated, don't-shine-too-brightly version of me.

Me.

And something about being seen that clearly,

by someone that rigorous,

in a room I had earned my place in,

gave the permission somewhere to land.

Not because I hadn't been told before.

Mrs. Griffin had told me in third grade.

The difficult English teacher had tried to tell me in her own hard way.

The world had been handing me evidence for decades.

But this time —

this classroom,

this season,

this version of me —

the soil was ready.
I opened my mouth.
I answered the question.
Not tentatively.
Not with the upward inflection that turns a statement into a request for approval.
Just —
answered it.
Like a woman who knew the answer.
Because I did.
And the world didn't end.
My voice didn't get me in trouble.
Nobody humiliated me for knowing too much.
Nobody called me cute and waited for the explosion.
Nobody sent me back to my place.
I just —
answered.
And sat with the strange, quiet, revolutionary feeling
of having used my voice
and found it was safe.
That's what the first time actually looks like.
Not a speech.
Not a stage.
Not a moment anyone else would mark on a calendar.
Just a woman in a classroom
giving herself permission
to know what she knows
out loud.
Mrs. Griffin planted the seed.
The world spent years trying to convince me the soil was wrong.

And one ordinary day in a graduate classroom,
something took root anyway.
Thirty years late.
Right on time.

Chapter 13

The Invitation Back to Myself

My father used to tell me I was the glue of the family.

He meant it as a compliment.

And I received it as one, for years.

But somewhere in my healing, I started turning that word over in my hands.

Glue.

Glue doesn't get to rest.

Glue doesn't get to fall apart.

Glue doesn't get to have needs.

Glue doesn't get to say, "I'm tired of holding this together."

Glue just holds.

And holds.

And holds.

Until it dries out.

I'd been the glue in my family, in my friendships, in my workplaces, in rooms where I didn't even know how I'd ended up responsible for the temperature.

The calm voice when someone else was losing it.

The comforter when someone needed steadying.

The problem solver when nobody asked me to solve anything.
The one who made sure everyone else was okay
while never once asking if I was.
It never even occurred to me to ask.

Healing is funny.
Not "ha ha" funny. More like "wow, I really used to stress myself out for absolutely no reason" funny.
I spent years trying to become a better version of myself,
only to realize the real work was unlearning everything that taught me to doubt who I already was.
It wasn't reinvention.
It was retrieval.
Me, finding me.
And the first sign that something was shifting wasn't confidence.
It wasn't a bold declaration or a dramatic boundary or a room I walked into differently.
It was curiosity.
Not the childhood kind where I asked a million questions and exhausted every adult in a five-mile radius.
This was quieter.
This was me turning the questions on myself —
not to interrogate,
but to investigate.
Not *What's wrong with me?*
But *What if nothing is?*
Nobody prepares you for how disorienting that shift is.
When you stop interrogating yourself
and start investigating the stories you inherited,
things get interesting real quick.

I looked around at everything I was carrying
and asked, for the first time in my life:
Who asked me to hold all of this?
I wasn't an over-apologizer.
I was an over-responsible child who had grown into an over-responsible adult.
Classic middle child.
Always mediating.
Always smoothing things over.
Always carrying the emotional weight in every room like it was my assigned seat —
as if someone had written my name on it before I arrived.

For most of my life I was the solution.

Not just because I arrived that way, ready, capable, already reaching for the problem before anyone had finished explaining it. But because I had shown up as the answer for so long that it became my persona. People knew they could call me. And they did. For money, for emotional labor, for practical help, for problems that were fully theirs to solve but had somehow found their way into my hands.

You'd be surprised how many people asked for money specifically. It happened more than once. More than a few times.

I said yes for years.

Not because anyone forced me. Because it felt like the right thing to do. My responsibility. The middle child, the glue, the one who held things together, she didn't get to have limits.

Until a relative I had recently met, barely knew really, asked to borrow money.

I was appalled.

And I said no.

And then I waited for what always came next.

In the years before, saying no would conjure a particular blend of guilt, sadness, and second-guessing that could follow me for days. There were times I had cried after saying no. Not because I regretted the decision. Because I was so braced for the consequences to that person that I took them on preemptively, carrying weight that was never mine to carry.

Each no before this one had still brought a few seconds of the old thoughts.

This time: nothing.

Just clarity.

I saw, without drama and without doubt, that this was not mine to do. And I didn't have to carry it.

The silence after the no was clean.

That was new.

That was everything.

I was in my late forties. The spa was signed. The work was done, or at least well underway. And somewhere in that season, without fanfare, without anyone handing it to me, I stopped being the person who cried after protecting herself.

I just became the person who knew the difference between love and depletion.

And chose accordingly.

I was carrying responsibilities that belonged to other people.

Trying to fix situations I didn't cause.

Trying to maintain peace I didn't disturb.

Trying to hold together people who were fully capable —

had always been fully capable —

of holding themselves.

And I had robbed them of the chance to do it

by always getting there first.

When I put some of that weight down —
even briefly,
even imperfectly —
two feelings arrived back to back so fast I almost missed the
first one.
Guilt.
The swift, familiar kind.
The kind conditioned into a girl who learned early that her
job was to make things easier for everyone around her.
The kind that whispers, *If you stop holding this, it will fall.*
And then, before the guilt could fully settle —
relief.
Pure.
Quiet.
Overdue.
The kind of relief that has been waiting patiently for years
while you were too busy being useful to notice it standing there.
Not because I stopped caring.
I will never stop caring.
But because I started caring about myself too —
in the same full, attentive, no-strings way I had always cared
for everyone else.
One ordinary day, I caught myself being kind to myself.
Not kind for the sake of it.
Not "treat yourself and move on" kind.
Not "I'll post about self-care and then go right back to over-
functioning" kind.
Actual kindness.
Softness.
Grace.
The kind of internal voice you'd use with a child who is trying
something hard for the first time —

patient, encouraging, not keeping score —
instead of the drill-sergeant tone I had used on myself for
most of my life.

I didn't announce it.

I didn't post it.

I didn't even say it out loud.

I just noticed that I had done something imperfectly
and hadn't spent the next three hours replaying it.

Here is what that looks like in practice.

I am in a meeting or on a call and someone uses a term I don't
recognize. The old version of me felt that moment like a small
alarm. A flicker of exposure. I would hold my face completely
still, nod at the right intervals, and the second that meeting
ended I would be in my car or back in my office looking it up.
Immediately. Urgently. As if not knowing was a deficit that
needed correcting before anyone could find out.

Now I write it down.

I circle a capital D next to it. D for define. My own private
system, the lifelong learner who never stopped being curious,
just finally stopped punishing herself for not already knowing
everything.

And then I get to it when I get to it.

If I look it up that evening, great.

If it sits in the notebook for three weeks, that's fine too.

My worth was never measured by the vocabulary I walked
into a room with.

I know that now.

Here's what strikes me about all of it.

The judgment I passed on myself in moments like that, the
urgency, the shame, the need to fix it immediately, I would
never apply any of that to another person. Not once. Not even

for a second. If a colleague hadn't known a term in a meeting I wouldn't have given it a second thought. If a friend had sent an email with the wrong their, I wouldn't have filed it away as evidence of anything.

I extended that grace to everyone.

Everyone except me.

For most of my life I was the harshest critic of the one person I should have been championing most.

That's over now.

I had just… moved on.

Like a person who believed she was allowed to be human.

Like a person who didn't have to earn her own grace.

I wasn't becoming myself.

I was returning to myself.

Quietly. Steadily. Without ceremony.

The way a woman moves when she has stopped running and started trusting where her own feet are taking her.

Healing wasn't the invitation.

I was the invitation.

My life was just catching up.

Chapter 14

What Healing Actually Looked Like — Not the Instagram Version

People make healing look glamorous.

Soft filters, matching journals, aesthetically pleasing quotes in perfect handwriting,

and captions about "stepping into my highest self."

That was not my healing.

Let me show you what mine looked like.

A local fundraiser. Dancing with the Stars format: community business owners paired with professional dancers, raising money for domestic violence awareness.

Someone asked if I wanted to participate.

I said yes.

Not after scanning the room for danger. Not after calculating the odds. Not after consulting the inner voice that had spent decades filing objections.

Just yes.

Clean. Fast. First.

And then I found the reasons to keep it. The cause was near to my heart in ways I didn't need to explain to anyone in that room. Domestic violence wasn't abstract to me.

So yes. Without hesitation.

Then I learned I could choose the genre. The music. That I could choreograph the routine myself, which was unusual for this format, where the professional typically drives the creative process. My pro partner trusted me enough to hand me the wheel.

Something I hadn't felt in years arrived when I heard that.

I cried.

Not from fear. Not from nerves.

From the absence of them.

I noticed, actually noticed, that the usual static wasn't there. The scanning. Every move weighed. The voice that had followed me into every room requiring something of me, whispering: Don't mess up. You're not as good as the others. Try harder to look like you belong here.

Quiet.

I chose Lewis Capaldi's "Before You Go."

I didn't overthink it. I just knew.

The first time I tried on my costume, I was not prepared for my reaction.

I looked in the mirror.

The body I'd had as a dancer was long gone. The extra weight, the years, the mileage. There it all was.

And then, almost immediately, before the old voice could even clear its throat:

I just didn't give a damn.

So what.

My dance partner and I were going to kill it. I knew it in my bones the way I used to know things before I learned to doubt myself out of everything.

I hadn't danced in front of anyone in decades.

My daughters had never seen me dance at all.

They didn't know this version of me existed. The one with the lifts and the stunts and the lyrical lines that come from a body that remembers what it was trained to do even when the mind has forgotten to be afraid.

We took the floor.

And we killed it.

I did the lifts. I did the stunts. I moved the way I used to move before I decided that moving like that was asking for too much attention.

My daughters were shocked.

Not because I was good.

Because I was free.

And honest looks good on me.

That's what healing actually looked like. Not the Instagram version. Not curated or cute. Not a straight line. Not pretty. And definitely not quick.

Healing looked like work.

Real work. Messy work.

The kind that makes you stare at the ceiling and say, "Okay… so we're doing this?"

Healing looked like realizing half the things I thought were my personality were actually protective tactics.

People thought I was naturally easygoing.

No.

I just knew what happened when people got upset.

People thought I was naturally strong.

No.

I didn't feel like I had permission to fall apart.

People thought I was naturally accommodating.

No.

I learned early that peace in the room often depended on me.

Healing meant sorting out what was actually me from what was trained into me.

Uncomfortable, necessary, and freeing in a way I hadn't expected.

Healing looked like catching myself mid-spiral and saying,

"We're not doing this today."

Sometimes out loud, sometimes in a whisper, sometimes in a full conversation with myself in the car.

I became my own gentle interrupter —

the voice that stepped in before the old patterns could finish their sentence.

Healing looked like noticing I was shrinking

and choosing not to.

The first time I caught it, it was subtle.

No one else would've noticed.

But I did.

I felt myself about to soften, minimize, make myself smaller to keep someone else comfortable.

To avoid being seen too clearly.

To avoid triggering someone else's insecurity.

Then something steadier rose up in me and said,

"You don't have to disappear to keep the peace."

And I didn't.

Do you know how powerful it is

to watch yourself stop abandoning yourself?

Everything changes.

Healing looked like discovering I wasn't quiet —

I was at peace.

There's a difference.
Quiet is shrinking.
Peace is ownership.
For the first time,
I wasn't scanning the room for danger, preparing for impact, rehearsing every word before I said it, tensing for someone else's reaction.
My mind was still enough
for me to hear myself.
Healing didn't make me softer.
It made me steadier.
I didn't become a new person.
I became the truest version of the person I had always been —
before fear, pressure, and early experiences
taught me to put everyone else first
and call it strength.

Chapter 15

The Expectations Nobody Agreed To

I was twelve years old.

My father had stomach issues his entire life and used to drink tall steins of milk throughout the day to coat it. My mother never hesitated to tell him he was wrong about something. This time, she did it in front of us.

He said, "What did you say?" Veins in his neck, tight. Eyes bulging with rage — self-righteousness, indignation.

He threw the stein of milk in her face.

I can still see it. The thick milk hesitating — then sliding down her face.

She didn't flinch.

She responded calmly. It was impressive.

She simply raised her hand and wiped it away.

That was that.

My mother was not passive. She started plenty of their fights and didn't back down from a single one. She was not a woman who absorbed things quietly.

They always fought behind closed doors. Her futile attempt to insulate us from it.

Didn't work. We have ears.

But this — this was not behind a closed door. I had positioned myself to jump in. Waiting for what always came next.

It never came.

She just wiped the milk away. And that was somehow more powerful than anything that could have followed.

I stood there frozen in disbelief and made a decision that would shape the next decade of my life:

I will never let a man treat me this way. I'm never getting married!

It's interesting — my mother had made her own vow years earlier. Hers was that when she married, she'd never divorce. We were standing in the same storm. We just chose different shelter.

I gave everyone else what I never gave myself.

Compassion. Grace. The benefit of the doubt. The assumption that people were doing their best with what they had, that their failures were understandable, that their wounds explained their behavior.

I extended that generosity freely, automatically, to almost everyone in my life.

Everyone except me.

For myself I kept a different standard. Harder. Less forgiving. The kind of internal voice that cataloged every misstep, questioned every instinct, and held my reactions up to a light so harsh that nothing could survive the scrutiny.

I didn't know I was doing it.

The ways we wound ourselves don't feel like wounds. They feel like standards. Like being realistic. Like not having illusions about who you are.

It took years of healing work to understand that the voice I was hardest on was the one that needed the most grace.

But before I got there, I got married.

The night we met, I wasn't looking for him.

I wasn't looking for anyone.

My college roommate had introduced me to a friend from Orlando who was stationed at Andrews Air Force Base. She dragged me to the NCO club that night. I wasn't much of a partier and definitely not on military bases. I'd had a decent enough time but I was ready to go.

We were seated at our table, which gave a clear view of the entrance. She asked if I was ready to leave. I turned to her, enthusiastic: *yes.* Positioned my body to get up, turned back toward the entrance —

And there he was.

Tall. Dark. Handsome. Dressed impeccably in a tailored suit. *Who. Is. That.*

I turned to her: "Girl, let me go get this brother's number and then we can leave."

I turned back. He'd disappeared into the crowd.

"Please. Give me a second to go find this guy."

I moved to stand — and he was already there. Standing right at my table. Asking me to dance.

My friend playfully pushed me toward him.

His version of that night is the one that still gets me.

He'd only been in DC about a month, newly transferred from a base in Japan. He and his buddy had been out all evening, hitting multiple clubs, enjoying the robust DC nightlife. On the drive back toward base housing, his buddy gave him the option: call it a night or check out the NCO club.

Reggie looked up at the full moon and something came over him.

God is going to send me my wife tonight.
NCO club it is.

He says I was the first person he saw coming through the door. As if there were a spotlight on me.

History.

He didn't try anything that night.

We just talked.

All night.

That may not sound like much. But for a woman who had spent her entire life calibrating how much of herself was safe to show, a man who wanted nothing but her words was everything.

I was twenty. He was twenty-one.

We were babies.

I'd been certain, for most of my life, that I'd never marry. Not quietly certain; loudly, comfortably, everybody-knows certain. Not against it for others. I could see its beauty from the outside. But from where I stood, having watched love up close, the joy of it and the devastation of it occupying the same house, sometimes the same evening, marriage was simply not for me. I'd had no shortage of viable suitors. There were good guys along the way, the kind who treated me well. I just wasn't available in the way that mattered. I kept them just far enough away to stay safe.

That's the thing about experiencing two people as they fight to love each other. It doesn't just show you what marriage is. It shows you what you're afraid it might be.

And I'd been avoiding it, shielding myself from it, for a long time.

Not hiding. Vigorously declining.

That tells you everything about how certain I had been.

So when I chose him — when I actually let someone in — it was not a casual thing. It was the bravest thing I had done since walking out of a kindergarten classroom at four years old.

Not all the way. Not immediately. But more than I had let anyone in before. I lowered the guard, that careful, calibrated, always-scanning guard I'd been building since I was old enough to understand that the world required careful navigation, and I said, in the way you say things without saying them: I trust you.

When Reggie and I announced we were getting married, my parents thought we were joking. My father actually laughed out loud.

"What — **CeWyon** is getting married?"

I understood completely. I had been the most vocal person in any room about never doing this exact thing. Watching me announce it with a straight face was funny. I'll give him that.

Once they realized we were serious, they were thrilled.

Of course they were. Their good days together were magnificent. The love was never in doubt. It was everything that lived alongside it that had taught me what I thought I knew about marriage.

The man I married is genuinely one of the most giving people I have ever known.

Not as a performance. Not selectively. As a way of being in the world.

His love language is acts of service and he speaks it fluently, constantly, without being asked. If something needs doing, Reggie does it. If someone needs help, Reggie shows up. He goes out of his way the way other people breathe — naturally, without calculation, without keeping score.

One of our first dates was picking up his newly purchased motorcycle.

That should tell you everything about who he is and why I fell for him. Not dinner and flowers. A motorcycle. We bonded over adventure, over movement, over the shared conviction that the world is worth going out into. We have always had fun together. That part has never been complicated.

We dated for nearly five years before we married — me just shy of twenty-six, him freshly twenty-seven. Within three months we were expecting our first child. Taylor arrived one week after my twenty-seventh birthday, two weeks late, and we were so ready for her to get here.

We had done everything right. The prep courses. The books. The research. We were prepared.

And then they told him to bring the car around.

I'm sorry — you're letting us take her home? By ourselves?

We were absolutely petrified. We fondly laugh about it now. But in that moment, standing in that hospital with this tiny person who had no idea she'd been assigned to two people who suddenly had no idea what they were doing — we were terrified in the most beautiful way.

By the time Reagan arrived nearly six years later, two weeks early this time, we were seasoned pros.

We were young. We were all in. And we were always going to be okay on the big things.

We are, in many ways, opposites. And in the ways that matter most: values, vision, what we believe a life should look like, how we want to show up in the world — *we* have always been the same.

My college roommate watched our relationship from the very beginning. Through the courtship, through the marriage, through thirty years of friendship.

Over those decades, she said the same thing more times than I can count: she had never seen two people speak to each other the way Reggie and I did. With that much kindness. That much care. That consistently, across that many years.

She meant it as admiration.

And she was right.

We were genuinely tender with each other. That was not an act. Not a performance. Not the careful, calibrated version of fine I had perfected in every other room of my life. With Reggie, the kindness was real. It was our default. It was the thing we returned to after every argument, every hard season, every stretch of silence that carried more weight than either of us understood.

People saw that and called it couple's goals.

I understood why they said it. I just never loved hearing it. Because I knew something they didn't.

Tenderness can also be a place to hide.

When kindness is your default, when civility matters to you both because of the homes you came from, when you've both watched what happens when people stop being careful with each other, you protect the gentleness at all costs. You guard it. You choose it again and again, even on the days it takes everything you have.

And underneath that choice, so far beneath the surface that neither of us could see it for years, something else was building.

Not hatred. Never that.

Not indifference. We were never indifferent.

A slow, quiet, white-hot resentment that had no language and no exit, because the two people carrying it loved each other too much to risk what honesty might cost.

We didn't fight often. When we did, it would eke out, a glimpse of what lived underneath, and then the tenderness would return, quickly, like a hand smoothing a wrinkle from a tablecloth. Not too much at a time. Not for long. Just enough to remind us both that something was there. And then we'd fold it back under.

Through the work, my work, his work, our work, we learned what we'd been doing.

We had been leading with our egos. With wounds we hadn't identified, let alone healed. With immaturity and stubbornness and, if I'm being honest, a kind of obstinance that only two people who are genuinely good at their core can sustain, because we believed our goodness exempted us from our blindness.

It didn't.

We were innately good people making poor choices. Reacting badly. Loving deeply and clumsily in the same breath.

We were not yet versed in giving each other unconditional positive regard. We didn't know that term. We didn't know it was missing. We just knew that something wasn't landing the way it should between two people who cared this much.

We matured together. Not at the same pace; that would have been too convenient, and nothing about us has ever been convenient. But together. In the same direction. Toward the same understanding.

I would not want to do this dance with anyone else.

Not because it's been easy. Because he is the only person on earth who knows every version of me, the dimmed one, the running one, the terrilluminated one, the one who signed a lease with shaking hands, the one who cried in a parking lot, the one who carried secrets for decades, the one who is writing all of it down right now.

And I know every version of him.

The parts we're proud of. The parts we've had to forgive. The parts we each shudder at the thought of anyone else knowing exist.

We know them.

And we're both still here.

That is not couple's goals. That is two people who refused to let go of each other long enough to figure out how to hold on better.

And with that trust came something I had no idea was there. An expectation.

Unspoken. Unarticulated. Never discussed. Never agreed to.

The expectation that he would protect me.

Not from physical danger. From the particular kind of hurt that comes when someone chooses someone else's comfort over your dignity. When the room is managed instead of defended. When the peace is kept at your expense.

His love was real. And it was everywhere. Extended to me, yes — but also to everyone around us. The same going-out-of-his-way, the same quiet acts of service, the same warmth. For me. For others. With equal generosity.

And I needed something more specific than generosity.

I needed to feel *chosen.* Defended. The particular kind of protected that means: *my dignity before this room's comfort. My peace before everyone else's ease.* The kind of love that sometimes has to disappoint the crowd to show up for the one.

He kept the peace instead.

Not because he didn't love me. Because keeping everyone comfortable felt, somewhere deep in him, like what love required.

And I would feel it like a fist to the chest.

Abandoned.

Betrayed.

Unloved.

Unimportant.

The feelings were real. The hurt was genuine. What I didn't understand then, couldn't understand then, was where it was actually coming from.

I just knew how I felt.

I didn't know I was feeling 1974.

I was feeling every moment when someone should have come and didn't. The community that watched and went back inside. The teachers who let me fall asleep at my desk without asking why. The adults who managed the image of the family while the children inside it learned that no one was coming.

I had spent my whole life being the one who showed up for everyone else. The glue. The middle child. The solution. The person who made sure everyone was okay while never once asking if I was.

And then I found someone I trusted enough to stop doing that with.

And I needed him to show up the way no one ever had.

But I couldn't tell him that.

Because I didn't know that's what I needed.

You cannot ask for what you don't yet understand you need. You cannot explain a wound you haven't faced. You can only feel the absence of something you never had words for, and wonder why the hurt is so disproportionate, so old-feeling, so much bigger than the moment that triggered it.

So I felt it alone.

And he kept the peace.

And neither of us understood what was actually happening.

We were both showing up broken in ways neither of us could see yet. Unspoken needs that became unmet expectations that hardened, over time, into something that looked like contempt but never actually was. When we didn't like each other — and there were seasons — it was never really about each other. It was about the gap. The place where we kept almost reaching each other and missing.

We both always knew we could never *not* like each other.

That knowledge was the rope we held onto through every season of missing.

The healing changed that.

Not in a single conversation. Not in a dramatic revelation. But gradually, as I did the work, the research, the therapy, the slow and unglamorous process of tracing my patterns back to where they started, I began to find the language.

And once I had the language, I could speak.

Not in the moment of hurt. Retroactively. In the way you explain something to someone who loves you and wanted to understand all along but didn't know there was something to understand.

Here's what's been happening in me.

Here's where it comes from.

Here's what I needed when you kept the peace instead of taking my side.

He heard it.

And he stepped up.

Imperfectly. Not always. Thirty-five years in, it still rears its head occasionally, the old pattern, the old hurt, the old feeling of standing alone in a room where someone should have come and didn't.

But it's different now.

He knows the wound. And because he knows it, he shows up differently. And because he shows up differently, I don't need it the same way. The wound doesn't run the relationship anymore.

That's what healing looks like in a marriage.

Not fixed. Not resolved once and never again.

Just two people who understand each other well enough to meet in the right place.

The same question that unlocked my story unlocked us.

What happened to you.

My "what the heck is wrong with this man" evolved into "of course he'd feel that way."

I can accept his flaws because of my own. Understanding how what happened to you shapes you has not only saved me — it is the number one sustaining factor in keeping this marriage intact. I get him now. And because I get him, I can give grace. Even when it doesn't feel good in that moment.

That's not settling.

That's what love actually looks like when two people do the work.

Thirty-five years.

We're still here.

And we still pick up motorcycles together.

Chapter 16

The Hearts I Sent Into the World

I went into motherhood with one non-negotiable.

Not a parenting philosophy. Not a discipline strategy. Not a list of milestones or a vision board of who they would become.

One thing.

They would know they belonged.

Not just in our home. Everywhere. In every room. At every table. In every moment when the world might try to make them feel like too much or not enough or somehow difficult to accommodate.

I had lived that feeling for decades. I knew its weight and its toll and the particular way it settles into a child's bones when nobody names it or challenges it or tells them the truth.

My daughters would not carry that.

Not if I could help it.

I won't pretend the road to them was easy.

Between Taylor and Reagan, we lost five pregnancies.

Five times we hoped. Five times we grieved. Five times I had to find a way to keep going while also keeping it together for the daughter who was already here, watching, absorbing everything she saw.

Taylor was around three during the first loss. We were sitting in an airport, waiting for a flight, and she looked at me with the particular attention of a child who notices everything. She reached up and took my face in her small hands.

You look so pretty when you smile like that, Mommy.

Two flight attendants nearby witnessed it. One said, "Mom, if you don't cry, we'll cry for you."

She was three years old. She had already learned to mirror love back to the people who needed it.

After the fourth loss, we decided to tell her about the baby being needed more by the angels. From that point on, her nightly prayer became:

God, please send me a baby brother or sister. And please don't take them back to Heaven this time.

I dissolved into a sobbing mess every single night.

And I questioned myself, whether telling her was the right thing to do, whether I was putting too much on those small shoulders. But Taylor had already decided she was in this with us. She had already made it her prayer. There was no protecting her from something she had already chosen to carry.

When Reagan finally arrived, Taylor was five and a half.

I asked her how she felt.

She said: I feel so, I feel so, and then she stopped, because existing words weren't enough for what was in her, and she invented a new one.

Congratulant.

I can still see that little snaggletoothed smile, wide as the ocean.

That word is in the dictionary of our family now. Permanent. Hers.

Taylor had always been observant, verbal, nuanced in ways that far exceeded her years. She felt things deeply and found words for all of it, even when she had to make them up.

Reagan was different from the beginning.

She arrived early but did everything else in her own time. First words, first steps, first opinions, all on her own schedule, thank you very much. When she finally did speak, it was in complete sentences. Her first recorded words were directed at her sister:

"Tayla." You are not the boss of me.

No preamble. No build-up. Just Reagan, fully formed, announcing the terms.

She's always been like that. A soul that felt like it had been here before. A child of few words whose words, when they came, were worth every moment of waiting. Wise in a way that made you pause. Profound in a way that made you take notes.

I raised two people who could not be more different from each other and, honestly, from me.

I have never met a stranger. I will talk to anyone, anywhere, about anything, and I suspect my daughters quietly talk trash about this behind my back. I think it's hilarious. I also think they're right.

I went into motherhood afraid. Genuinely, almost debilitatingly afraid. Afraid that I would say the wrong thing, do the wrong thing, pass something down that I hadn't finished healing. That I would look up one day and see in their eyes the particular look of a child who doesn't feel seen.

I told them that.

Not once. Consistently, over years, in the way that becomes its own kind of language between a mother and her daughters. I was transparent about the fear, about the work, about what I was learning and unlearning. They grew up knowing their mother was human. That she was trying. That she was afraid of hurting them and doing it anyway, showing up anyway, choosing them anyway.

They know about this book. None of it will surprise them.

Some of it they're hearing for the first time.

I apologized when I was wrong. When my delivery was too sharp or my anger landed somewhere it didn't belong. My parents never did that. I knew from the beginning it would not be me. I chose not to use corporal punishment. Instead I helped them connect the dots between choices and consequences. I let them feel disappointment but taught them how to process it. And I taught them to give themselves grace.

That last one took me fifty years to learn.

I handed it to them as a baseline.

There were moments I overcorrected. My husband saw it before I did. There was the car. Our oldest had done everything we asked, and I wanted to buy her a car that matched her effort and, if I'm honest, that matched what the other kids were driving. I didn't want either of my girls to feel othered. Not for a single moment. Not for any reason.

Reggie was right. I told him so.

That instinct came from somewhere real. From roll call and mispronunciations and brown faces in rooms full of other faces. I had absorbed the toll of not belonging so thoroughly that I was willing to overspend to spare them a version of it. He helped me see the difference between protection and compensation. I received that.

I wanted them to chart their own courses. That was non-negotiable. Whoever they were, whatever they wanted, I would cheer from whatever sideline they chose.

I'll be honest: I had hoped, somewhere in the quiet of my own heart, that one of them might love dance. Or performing arts. Music. The things that saved me. The language my body spoke before I had any other language.

Neither of them was interested.

And I cheered from the gymnastics sidelines and the volleyball sidelines and the softball sidelines and the soccer sidelines as if they were dancing Swan Lake at the Atlanta Ballet.

Because it was never about me.

It was about them.

Taylor is the litigator. Of course she is. The child who negotiated with God, who invented vocabulary for joy, who always found the exact right word, she grew up to argue for other people's rights in a courtroom. She was always going to end up somewhere that required language and precision and the kind of empathy that walks into a room and immediately understands what's at stake.

Reagan just graduated from undergrad and is working in commercial property management, leaning toward development. Building things. Deciding what gets built and where. The child who did everything in her own time, who spoke when she was ready and said something worth hearing, she's going to build spaces where people live their lives. That tracks completely.

We are poised to support wherever our girls' dreams take them. Prepared to show it. With presence, with guidance, and yes, with financial backing. They are well worth the investment.

They came into this world as themselves. I just tried not to get in the way of that.

I didn't always succeed. But I showed up. I apologized. I kept trying.

And somewhere in that trying, something changed, not in me, but in what I was able to give them. The thing I spent fifty years learning to give myself, I handed to them before they ever needed to spend fifty years without it.

They know they belong.

They know they are enough.

They know their mistakes don't define them and their fear doesn't have to stop them.

They know their mother was afraid and did it anyway.

And they know, because I told them, that they are the best thing I have ever done.

It's as if someone plucked out my heart and attached legs to it.

And sent it into the world twice.

Chapter 17

Showtime and Chappy

Before I tell you who they were to each other, let me tell you who they were.

James Henry Chandler was born on February 26, 1936, in Winter Park, Florida — delivered at home on 225 W. Lyman Avenue by Dr. Wells, with the help of a midwife. His parents were Charles and Annie Chandler, known to their family as Papa Charles and Mother Dear.

Papa Charles had his own origin story. He ran away from home in Georgia at twelve years old — hopped trains until he decided, for reasons only he ever fully understood, to disembark in Winter Park. He was of mixed race, and tough in the way that people become tough when tenderness was never modeled for them. My father had no memory of Papa Charles ever telling him he loved him.

Not once.

What that does to a child — the slow, quiet accumulation of a love that is present but never spoken — is its own kind of wound. One that doesn't announce itself. One that just shapes the man.

And then Mother Dear left.

She took the other children with her. Jamesy stayed behind.

He was young enough that the reasons didn't matter — only the fact of it did. The fact that when she went, he wasn't the one she took. That wound settled into him early and deep, the way wounds do when there's no language yet to name them and no one to help carry them.

She came back. But by then, something had already been decided in him.

He grew up charming, mischievous, magnetic — a man who filled every room he entered. Mercurial, with an advanced command of four-letter words. His tongue was equally as acerbic as it was smooth. A world-class sweet talker or a world-class cusser, depending entirely on the day you caught him.

He was drum major at Hungerford School, leading the marching band with the kind of authority that only he fully believed he had. His sister Teedum was a majorette. The power struggle between them for control of that band was legendary — and very likely her way of getting him back for every moment he had delighted in aggravating her as a child.

His father insisted he learn a trade. So James enrolled at Florida A&M in Tallahassee and studied to become a licensed barber. He was good at it. Then he became exceptional at it. In the early 1980s, he opened his flagship business: Chappy's Barber Shop — white leather couches, a brick indoor wishing well, red walls and carpets. Unheard of for a barbershop at the time. It was once voted the Best Barbershop in Florida. He operated it for over forty years.

He gave a mean fade. He was quick with advice, quicker with a comeback. His clients knew better than to sit in his chair when he was hungry — he had no hesitation setting down his clippers mid-cut to enjoy his dinner while you waited, half-finished, in the chair.

James "Chappy" Chandler made his mark in ways that were impossible to miss. He fathered ten children.

He spent his whole life trying to fill something that had been empty since he was too young to name it.

He was, as I would eventually come to understand, doing exactly what the unhealed version of any of us does.

The best he could with what he had been given.

Frankye Marie Grant was born on July 22, 1950, in Ocala, Florida — in her mother's family's multigenerational home — and raised in Orlando. Her parents were Frank Grant Sr. and Rosa Lee Thomas Grant, known to everyone who loved them as Sporty Boy and Peaches.

Sporty Boy earned his name the hard way. He grew up impoverished, often without shoes, and made a vow that when he was able, he would always wear the finest clothes and the best shoes. He kept that promise for the rest of his life. The man was impeccably dressed until the end.

Peaches earned hers differently. She danced — the Lindy Hop, the clubs, the music of an era. And when she walked down the street, white shopkeepers — remarkable for that time — would come out of their stores just to tell her she was beautiful. That her skin looked like peaches and cream. The name stuck.

When their marriage ended, Frankye was five years old.

She watched her family come apart and made a quiet, iron vow to herself: when she married, she would never divorce.

Rosa Lee worked multiple jobs to keep the household going. Often it wasn't enough. Sporty Boy tried to help — he sent what he could — but Rosa Lee, bitter at his indiscretions, wouldn't accept it. She would manage on her own terms or not at all.

By the time Frankye was grown, her parents had found their way back to cordial. Friendly, even. Rosa Lee remained close to members of Sporty Boy's family for the rest of her life. Time has a way of softening what pride hardens.

But in those early years, it was Frankye who held things together.

The oldest. The only daughter. She stood in the gap while her mother worked. She tended to her younger brothers. She assisted when her mother delivered her youngest siblings — not as a bystander, but as a participant, hands and presence and quiet competence, at an age when she should have had nothing more pressing than her own homework.

She grew up faster than any child should have to. Not because anyone asked her to. Because she could see what needed doing and she was the one who could do it.

That instinct never left her.

It just found new rooms to fill.

Rosa Lee supplemented the household by helping the performers who passed through Central Florida — babysitting their children when they came to town. In that era, with whites-only hotels locking doors that should have been open, artists stayed wherever they were welcomed. And so a little girl in Orlando found herself playing with the Turner children one minute — Ike and Tina's — and then transforming into something else entirely the next.

At fourteen, Frankye Grant was dubbed Little Miss Dynamite.

Not as a nickname. As a verdict.

Because when she stepped on that stage — cape on, signature spins ready, voice like something that had been waiting its whole life to be released — there was no other word for what she was.

She performed across Central Florida. She played clarinet in the school marching band. She made her own clothes. She drew. She designed. She coordinated. She created.

She was, as those who witnessed her would later agree, simply too much talent for any one life to contain.

She studied early childhood education at Seminole State College and went on to become an educator and administrator in Orange County Public Schools. She directed and choreographed drill team drum corps for the City of Winter Park and the City of Altamonte Springs.

She was nineteen when she married James Henry Chandler. He was thirty-six. She became his third wife.

By twenty-one, she had three babies under the age of four.

She had walked into something complicated with her eyes open — because she had been walking into things that required more than she should have had to give since she was five years old, and she had never once turned back.

That was Frankye Marie Grant Chandler.

James Henry Chandler — February 26, 1936 – July 17, 2021.

Frankye Marie Grant Chandler — July 22, 1950 – September 5, 2016.

They were my parents.

And this chapter is theirs.

My father's name was Chappy.

Not his given name. His name. The one that fit him the way his clothes fit him: sharp, deliberate, impossible to ignore.

He was handsome in a way that multiple generations noticed. My friends told me so, even when they were grown. He had been a drum major, and that was how my mother first spotted him, marching down the street in a parade. She was five years old. She watched him pass and decided, with the certainty only a five-year-old can muster, that he was going to be her husband.

It took her almost a decade to make that happen.

He could really, really dance. I loved watching my parents dance together. People would stop and stare admiringly, the way people stop for something worth seeing. He was equally as talented as my mother, except his art was a barber's chair, and he was a master at it. He gave generations their first haircuts, their special occasion cuts, their before-the-big-day cuts. He had a shotgun by that chair and didn't hesitate to threaten to use it.

I only learned in adulthood that this was why no one ever asked me out.

I had spent years wondering why no boys seemed interested. Meanwhile, Chappy had quietly terrorized an entire neighborhood into keeping their distance from his daughter.

That was my father.

He loved to go. He'd pile us into the car with no particular destination and we'd end up somewhere fun: the beach, wherever. I still call myself a go baby because of him. He taught me that the world was worth moving through, that good things were waiting if you just got in the car and pointed it somewhere.

He also set us up with a popcorn machine when we were in elementary school.

Our first business.

He had owned his own barbershop his entire life. Never worked for anyone else. He raised us to be little entrepreneurs, hauling our antique wares to Sunday afternoon shows, learning to sell, learning to negotiate, learning that your work could be your own if you wanted it badly enough.

I didn't connect those dots for a long time.

He had ten children.

Two before marriage. Two inside the first marriage. Three outside of it. None from his second, very brief marriage. And then us: Toddrick, CeWyon, and Cory, with my mother, his wife of more than thirty years before they finally separated. Neither ever remarried. Neither ever actually filed for divorce.

I once asked him why he had so many children.

He said he wanted Chandlers.

He got them. All ten showed up looking exactly like him. There was never any question about whose they were. Chappy made his mark and it arrived in ten faces that left absolutely no doubt.

I also asked him, at his bedside in his final weeks, why he had chased so many women.

He looked at me and said:

"I didn't chase women. Women chased me."

I said: "Did you have to let so many catch you?"

And he laughed.

Not defensively. Not with shame. With the unrepentant, easy charm that had always been his signature. And I laughed too, which was new. Before, I would have been seething having that conversation with him. The old anger would have risen, the old hurt, the old weight of everything his choices had snatched from my mother and our family.

This time there was airiness.

Because somewhere between the research and the therapy and the bedside questions I had never dared ask before, I had gotten the answer I was actually looking for.

Not the one about women.

The one about him.

He had a very challenging childhood. Attachment wounds that ran deep and never got named or treated. A little boy who grew into a man still trying to fill something that had been empty since before he understood what emptiness was.

What happened to him.

The same question that had unlocked my own story unlocked his.

I didn't excuse him. I understood him.

And understanding him, the full complicated brilliant difficult charming magnetic infuriating man, is its own kind of release.

There was one more thing about Chappy that deserves its own mention.

He was absolutely, unapologetically, magnificently vain.

Not privately. Openly. The way only a man completely unbothered by the contradiction could be.

He dyed his hair, his mustache, and his sideburns well into his seventies. He did push-ups and calisthenics through middle age and beyond. He used wrinkle creams. LED light therapy masks. Anything science or vanity had invented to hold back what time was coming for regardless.

My oldest brother Greg — my father's son from his first marriage, who officiated his funeral at my request, despite their complicated relationship — called him the youngest old person he'd ever known. That was exactly right.

Chappy was cool. He was hip. A natural byproduct of spending his entire life inside a barbershop — surrounded by the pulse of the culture, the sounds of the times, the latest trends and the oldest conspiracy theories, all circulating in the same room. The barbershop is the epicenter of the Black community. Chappy absorbed all of it. He never stopped.

He dated younger women. I never fully understood what drove that. I suspect he did.

And yet — there was one thing about him that defied all of it. His clothes.

The man was a snazzy dresser. Impeccable. Even when the occasion called for casual, Chappy showed up dressed to the nines. Collared button-downs and dress shoes to work. Every day. To a barbershop. That he owned. We teased him endlessly about his velvet suit jackets.

I had never seen him in jeans until he was well into his sixties. And even then, he dressed those up.

Shorts? Never. Not once.

He was notoriously slim his entire life and absolutely loathed what he called his bird legs and bony knees.

I thought about that when I wrote earlier about my own skinny bird legs — the ones I prayed would fill out, the ones I hadn't yet learned to love.

He gave me those legs.

We looked alike. But we couldn't have been more different.

We were driving down a road that ran alongside a lake.

Water skiers were cutting across the surface, jumping ramps like it was nothing.

I watched them for a moment.

Then said it out loud:

"When I get big, I'm going to be rich. I'm going to have a big boat and a mansion."

My parents' eyes met in a furtive glance.

Only my mom spoke.

Her voice was soft. Like she was trying to cushion something she knew might land hard.

"Baby, we're not rich. Our parents weren't rich. And you're not going to be rich either."

What I heard was:

not for you.

not your life.

not your future.

I nodded.

But inside, something in me stood up.

I don't know who they're talking about…

but I'm going to be rich.

The problem… and the possibility.

Both of them. Already. At eleven.

He died holding my hand.

The man who gave me my name, who gave me my first business, who taught me to go, who danced in a way that made strangers stop and stare, he left this world with his daughter's hand in his.

I had always thought I would be terrified of a deceased person. I wasn't. I stayed for two hours. I couldn't make myself leave the father I had spent a lifetime trying to understand and had only recently gotten to know.

I wept for the loss.

And I wept for the little boy.

The one who never got the question asked of him either.

"What happened to you, Chappy?"

Bless that child's heart.

At my mother's celebration of life, while the video montage played, the one I had assembled in five days, the one that included him even though they hadn't been together in years, because I knew she would have wanted it that way, he leaned over to me and said:

"Our little family sure did have a lot of fun together."

I was furious.

This from the man who had just spent an hour refusing to sign the cremation papers.

But I looked at him, this frail, vulnerable, still-charming version of the man I had always known as larger than life, and I thought:

"Yes, Chappy. We did."

I knew it was about to start before either of them raised their voices.

The air went still.

I could feel the explosion building before it ever arrived.

And something else rose with it, thick in my throat: regret…
and guilt.

Dang it. I've sparked a fight again.

My brothers and I shared dishwashing duty. Every week it
was the same argument about whose turn it was. No matter what
system we used, if there was any question, it somehow landed on
me.

I was standing at the sink, filling it with water.

"But it's not my—"

I didn't get the rest out.

Smack.

My head snapped to the side. Heat spread across my face
before I could even process what had happened.

In sixteen years, he had barely raised his voice at us. He didn't
have to. That tone was enough to bring me to tears.

But this time was different.

Cedric was visiting. My big brother, home on leave from the
Marines. We rarely got to see him. Having him in the house felt
special. The kind of occasion that should have been left alone.

Silence.

A full, suspended kind of silence.

Then everything broke.

*"Don't you EVER hit my beautiful sister in the face like that
again."*

Cedric's voice didn't rise. It dropped. Heavy. Final.

And then he moved.

In one motion, he had my father off the ground.

My chest tightened.

I didn't know where to look.

I didn't know who to protect.

My mom rushed between them.

Cedric shifted back just as quickly, like something in him snapped back into place.

My father tried to force him out.

And then it turned.

Onto my mother.

Again.

My heart pounded so hard I could hear it in my ears.

This is my fault.

"STOP!"

The word tore out of me before I could think about it.

"This is why I can't wait to get out of here. And once I leave, I am never coming back."

The room shifted again.

My mother turned toward him.

"Jamesy. You are running my daughter away. I will not let you do that."

That night stretched longer than it should have.

And the part that stayed with me wasn't the slap.

It was the feeling that I had done something to cause all of it.

That somehow, it had started with me.

Again.

I am always causing problems between my parents.

If I speak up, it makes things worse.

If I stay quiet, it still happens.

Somehow, it always comes back to me.

But nights like that weren't rare.

My father being too harsh.

My mother — or Todd, or Cory — stepping in.

The pattern was familiar enough that I learned how to move inside it.

Which is why it always confused me when people would tell me how much my father talked about his baby girl. How proud he was.

That version of him and the one I experienced in moments like this…

they didn't seem to belong to the same man.

I learned early that two things could be true at the same time.

That math never quite added up for me.

Not then.

Not until much later.

Not until the very end.

He was something else.

But he was my guy.

When I wrote his obituary, I chose two words that I believe captured him completely.

Perfectly imperfect.

And on his deathbed, he told me I was his favorite.

Not because I was the easiest. Because I held him accountable. Because I told him how I felt. Because I was a fierce protector of my mother and he knew it and he loved me for it.

I never knew that.

I had spent decades believing that being too honest, too fierce, too unwilling to look away was a liability.

My father died telling me it was the thing he loved most.

She was my girl. I didn't play about her. And she didn't play about me. Everyone knew it. Including him. I think that's exactly why he said what he said.

I called her Mommycakes.

Only me. That was mine.

She was striking in the way that made people notice. Not just glance, notice. Physically fit well into her senior years, with legs that people remarked on and she knew it, carrying them with the confidence of a woman who had made peace with her own beauty a long time ago.

Her signature was matching. Not just an outfit. Everything. Every color accessory you could name. Shoes in every shade, hundreds of pairs, a collection that suggested less a hobby and more a deeply held personal conviction. She went by Jackie — Frankye was reserved strictly for classmates — and her vanity plate said Lady C. And her nails. The shape of her nail beds was something manicurists stopped to admire out loud. I did too.

She'd walk into a room and eyes would go to her before she said a word.

I remember watching her as PTA president, standing at the front of a room full of adults, commanding the space with the full force of her considerable presence. Intelligent, eloquent, authoritative. A speaker who made you forget you hadn't planned to stay long. She could do anything. I knew it watching her. I was proud and I knew it.

The specific kind of pride that belongs only to a child watching her parent be magnificent.

And her laugh. Oh, that laugh. Melodic is the only word that comes close. The kind of laugh that was its own invitation, you didn't need to know what was funny. You heard it and you were already smiling, already leaning in, already gone. Her mother had the same laugh. It skipped generations the way the best things do.

She was a talker. And her stories were worth every word.

I am my Mommycakes' child.

I miss her voice. A smooth, soothing, rich tone that could fill a room without trying. Her singing was divine. But that speaking voice, what I wouldn't do to hear her call my name one more time.

My mother is the reason music lives in me the way it does. She taught us songs when we were small, the three of us piled together learning every word. "There Was a Mouse That Lived on the Hill" was our favorite. It has so many verses. We would sing them with her for what felt like hours, our little faces gleefully exaggerating every word, pantomiming every scene, delighting in the performance of it.

I can still see our faces.

She dressed us alike for years. All three of us, color coordinated, decked out, matching from head to toe. We couldn't stand it at the time.

Looking back at those pictures now, I get it completely. And I love it.

I dearly wish I'd had the presence of mind to record my bedside conversations with her in hospice, the way I did with my father five years later. By then I knew better. By then I understood that those conversations were irreplaceable. With her, I was still the one holding everything together, still moving, still doing what needed to be done. The presence of mind to press record didn't find me until it was too late.

That is one of the quiet griefs I carry.

She was a PE teacher with a gift for nicknames. If she called out to you, bring your happy hips over here, you knew she liked you. Her students knew it too.

She was co-director of community drum corps. She stayed up late making the majorettes' uniforms from scratch, every one of them, by hand, from nothing. And naturally, she tossed me into the mix early. I was barely out of toddlerhood marching in my first parade because my mother was the director and that's just how it went.

On good days, they rode bikes around the neighborhood with kids tagging along behind them. They played kickball and softball on the field right next to our house, right there with us, not watching from the sidelines. They were fun in the way that made the whole neighborhood come to them.

Our parents were a blast.

Until they weren't.

What I think of when I think of my mother is sacrifice.

She was determined that her children would grow up in a two-parent home. And that was that.

There was a day, we were in elementary school, when she and my father sat the three of us down. They were divorcing. She and the children would be moving to Atlanta. She'd been offered an opportunity to head a department at the Equitable Insurance Company. A real opportunity. A skyscraper.

We cried.

We begged.

We pleaded.

And they stayed.

It is one of the few regrets of my life.

Not because I was wrong to be a child who wanted her family together. I was a child. Children aren't supposed to carry that weight and we shouldn't have been given it. But I've carried it anyway, the understanding that our tears were part of what kept her in a house that was, all at once, violent and loving and dysfunctional and fun and happy and depressed for decades to come.

She had the skyscraper.

She chose the mouse song.

She had the skyscraper.

I will go to my grave convinced that given her multitudes of skills and her considerable talents, she could have been a formidable international fashion designer. A CEO. A famous singer. The stages were there. The gifts were undeniable. The world would have received her.

But she chose us.

I have spent years learning to hold both of those truths without letting either one crush the other.

We had two names for her.

Much Much Energy, for the days when the force of her filled every room before she even spoke.

And Showtime, for the moments she stepped out the door: clothes perfect, shoes right, looking like she knew the world was watching and had decided to give it something worth seeing.

My two brothers and I used both.

Depending on the day.

Both were true.

That was our mother.

She was intelligent and graceful and sometimes sad in ways nobody named until much later, when I learned the word bipolar and felt the particular ache of understanding something retroactively.

She could look at any gown in any magazine and recreate it without a pattern.

She turned down a chance to tour with Tina Turner because she didn't want to leave my father behind.

She was a teenager when they met.

She studied early childhood education and made us her test subjects, which is to say: she was paying attention to us with the full force of her considerable mind, always.

She had made a promise to her five-year-old self that she would never divorce. Her own parents had. She wasn't going to.

So she kept the promise, decade after decade, through everything, because she was the kind of woman who meant what she said to herself, even when she was five, even when keeping the promise was the hardest thing she'd ever done.

But before any of that, before the marriage, before us, before the promise had even been tested, there was a yellow Cadillac.

She was still a teenager, newly in love, when a friend spotted her driving my father's very distinctive, very flashy yellow Cadillac.

The friend asked if she was dating him.

She said yes.

The friend said: my mama has a baby with him.

My mother, taken aback, said: I want to meet her.

Not: I need to think about this. Not: that changes things. Not even a pause.

I want to meet her.

They pulled into the friend's mother's yard. Children were running everywhere, playing hide and seek. My mother scanned for a baby.

No luck.

Then a four-year-old girl who had been counting with her face hidden against a tree turned around.

My mother looked at her and said:

"That's her."

A mini copy of my father. Looking back at her.

My mother began picking her up. Bringing her around. Making sure we knew our big sister.

We adored her. She adored my mother. So much so that when my mother passed, my sister grieved as if my mother had given birth to her too.

My mother was a teenager when she did that.

That's who she arrived as.

Not who she became. Who she already was.

When we learned we were losing her, she said she wanted to go home.

Not to a facility. Not to a hospital. Home. To her siblings. To her tight-knit classmates. To her church. To the people who had known her longest and loved her most completely.

So I made it happen.

I negotiated with her physicians. Obtained permission to transport oxygen tanks. Found the specific tanks that regulations allowed. My husband drove seven hours from Atlanta to Orlando through a hurricane to help bring her home.

How fitting. A hurricane. Of course.

She arrived. She stayed longer than the doctors had prepared us for, which felt like exactly the right thing for a woman who had always exceeded expectations.

In the days before her medical supplies were delivered, I drained fluid from her lungs.

Into a bowl.

I wasn't okay. I knew I wasn't okay. But I kept moving because someone had to, and the middle child, the glue, the one who held things together because the situation required it. She was still in there, still doing what needed to be done.

My mother passed at home, the way she wanted.

And then I planned her homegoing.

I had five days.

I did not entrust even minor tasks to anyone else. I could not. Not because help wasn't offered. Because this was the last thing I could do for her, and I needed it to be right. I needed it to be seen. I needed it to be everything she was.

Showtime deserved a show.

So I built one.

Vignettes of her life, arranged like scenes in a play she would have directed herself. The child performer who commanded a stage at fourteen. The woman who chose love over the tour. The director of the drum corps, calling out steps, shoulders back, completely in her element. The fit middle-aged physical education teacher who carried herself like she knew the world was watching. And finally — because my father chose it, and I trusted him on this one thing — her as an angel, singing the song she loved most on stage.

Aretha Franklin's "Ain't No Way."

A song about a woman begging not to be shut out of someone's heart.

I don't think that was a coincidence. I think that was my mother telling the truth one last time, in the language she trusted most.

It was flawless.

And then it was over.

And I drove home.

And I walked into my bedroom.

And I stood in the stillness of a house that had held her and now didn't.

And I made a decision.

A conscious, deliberate, chosen decision. The kind only a woman who has done the work can make.

I gave myself permission to not be okay.

Not because I fell apart. Not because I couldn't hold it anymore.

Because I finally knew I was allowed to feel it.

The old version of me would have kept going. Would have found the next task, the next thing to manage, the next way to be useful. Would have processed her grief in stolen moments, privately, efficiently, without inconveniencing anyone.

This version stood still.

And let it come.

All of it. The slippers on the stairs. The pallet on the stranger's floor. The woman who came to me to process instead of to reassure. The complicated, lifelong, irreplaceable love of it. The fifty years of learning to hold her failures and her gifts in the same hand without either one crushing the other.

She was a teenager in a yard, scanning for a baby, who turned around and became her daughter's big sister.

And standing in that stillness, I understood what it means to go back for Little Me.

It means doing for her what no one did for you.

It means seeing what she carried.

It means giving your mother the sendoff she earned, every detail witnessed, nothing minimized — and then standing in the quiet afterward and letting yourself grieve without apologizing for the sound of it.

Chapter 18

The Day I Went Back for Little Me

I have a photograph of her.

Seven years old. Mrs. Griffin's class, the teacher who looked at my test scores and told me, as a fact, that I was smart. The same year I was recommended for the gifted program and never got on the bus.

She's wearing her favorite outfit: a pink blouse and a flowered skirt.

Her hair is big and beautiful, her mother had given her careful curls that morning, painstaking and loving, and Central Florida's humidity had undone every one of them on the walk to school.

She showed up anyway.

I've shown this photograph in my speeches. Held it up in rooms full of people and said, "This is who I'm talking about."

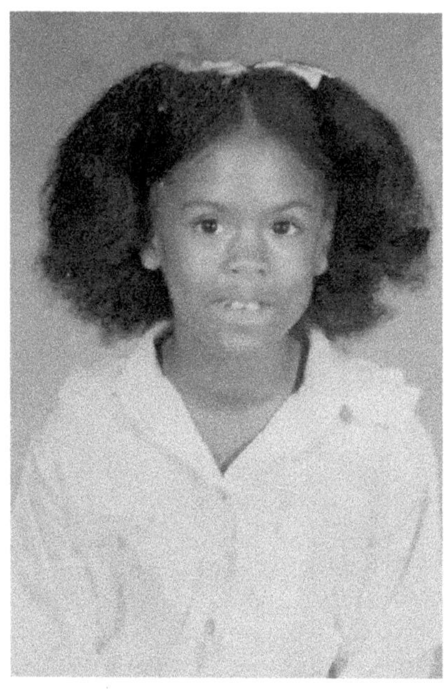

This is her.

She's looking at the camera the way she looked at everything, like she's deciding whether to trust it.

And she is, unmistakably, already herself.

There are moments in healing that feel less like reflection and more like reunion, the kind where your heart recognizes someone long before your mind catches up.

That's what it felt like the day I sat down with the little girl I used to be.

Not physically. But in that quiet internal space where truth does its best work and memory stops running from itself.

I closed my eyes, and there she was.

Tiny. Bright-eyed. High-pitched voice. Gently sucking her bottom lip, her built-in pacifier, the thing her body had found to self-soothe long before anyone thought to give her something else to hold onto.

Curious to the bone. Always thinking. Always watching. Always trying to make sense of a world that didn't make enough sense on its own.

My little Chick.

She didn't say a word. She just looked at me, wide-eyed and expectant, the way children look at the adults they hope can be trusted.

So I spoke gently. Softly. Like I was afraid of breaking something already fragile.

Sweetheart… none of this was your fault.

Her posture shifted, just a little, like she'd been carrying that sentence for thirty years and heard it put down.

My darling, you were never too much. You were never hard to love. You were never the reason somebody got angry or disappointed or overwhelmed. You were not the cause. You were the child.

You didn't deserve the silence you were bribed into. Or the confusion nobody helped you make sense of. Or the responsibility that landed on shoulders that were barely strong enough to hold a backpack.

You were just a baby. A brilliant one. An intuitive one. An honest one. And the world wasn't always gentle with you. That was never your doing.

I could feel her listening. Holding her breath. Taking in every word like she was afraid they might disappear if she looked away.

And then she asked it.

The question she had been carrying since before she had the words for it.

Why did this happen to me?

She looked straight at me when she said it. Not accusatory. Not angry. Just a child who had waited a very long time for someone to be honest with her.

Why are people so mean to me?

I didn't look away.

I didn't rush to fix it or soften it or redirect it.

I let the question land where it needed to land.

And then I told her the truth.

I wish I could tell you it makes sense. It doesn't. Some of it was circumstances you were born into that had nothing to do with you. Some of it was people carrying their own pain and not knowing where else to put it. Some of it was simply that your light was bright enough to make people notice, and not everyone knows what to do with that.

But hear what I'm saying:

None of it was a verdict on your worth.

None of it was proof that you were wrong to be exactly who you are.

And none of it, not one single moment of it, was your fault.

So I kept going. Because she needed to hear all of it.

My love, you were punished for the truth. You were scolded for being perceptive. You were teased for your light. You were misunderstood because you saw more, felt more, knew more than people expected from a child.

You didn't get in trouble because you were wrong. You got in trouble because you were accurate.

And that scared people.

You were inquisitive in a world that preferred obedience. You were expressive in a world that valued quiet. You were gifted in a world that didn't know how to nurture it.

You weren't a problem. You were a revelation. And revelations make people uncomfortable.

She looked up at me then, not skeptical, just unsure, the way a child looks when she wants to believe something but isn't ready to trust it fully.

I'm sorry. I'm sorry nobody protected your innocence. I'm sorry you carried secrets too heavy for your age. I'm sorry the adults around you didn't always know how to love you in the ways you needed most.

I'm sorry you learned so early that being yourself could cost you something.

I'm sorry no one told you that your name was beautiful. That your questions were brilliant. That your voice was necessary. That your truth was holy.

You deserved care. You deserved safety. You deserved gentleness. You deserved to be believed. You deserved to be guided with love.

And none of that was your responsibility to earn.

She blinked, slowly, like she was letting the words settle into the places where old hurts used to live.

You survived. You made it. Not because anyone showed you how, but because you were extraordinary before you ever understood the word.

You grew up to be wise. You grew up to be warm. You grew up to be fierce, even in the moments you felt fragile.

You became the kind of woman people turn to without thinking. The kind of woman who changes a room with presence alone. The kind of woman who leads from truth and loves from depth.

You became me.

And then I leaned in close, close enough that she could feel the certainty of it, and I said the things nobody ever said.

You are enough.

Not when you make yourself smaller. Not when you achieve. Not when you make yourself easy to love or easy to manage or easy to be around.

Right now. As you are. In this body. With this name that people couldn't be bothered to say correctly. With this voice that asks too many questions and this light that makes people uncomfortable.

You are enough.

And you are worthy.

Worthy of being protected. Worthy of being seen. Worthy of someone asking if you're okay and actually waiting for the answer. Worthy of taking up space without apologizing for it. Worthy of the love you have spent your whole little life pouring into everyone else.

You didn't have to earn any of it. You never did.

And these hard things you're in the middle of, and the ones coming after them, you are going to do them. Every single one. Not because no one else will. Because you are genuinely that capable.

But hear me.

You do not have to do them alone.

You were never supposed to do them alone.

Asking for help is not weakness. Needing someone is not a burden. Letting people carry something with you is not a failure of strength.

It is the thing I wish someone had told you before you decided, at an age when you should have been worrying about nothing more serious than spelling tests and Saturday cartoons, that your needs were the ones that could wait.

They couldn't wait.

You couldn't wait.

I'm here now. And I'm not going anywhere.

We're doing this together.

She looked at me for a long moment.

Gently sucking her bottom lip.

Thinking.

And then something in her face changed. Not all at once. The way dawn comes, so gradually you can't name the exact moment the dark became light.

She wasn't fixed.

She was seen.

And for a child who had spent so long being invisible in plain sight, being seen was enough to begin.

Thank you, my love. For being braver than you knew. For holding so much. For surviving what you didn't understand. For protecting us even when it wasn't fair.

You don't have to carry any of it anymore. I've got it now. You can rest, for now. I'll keep coming back. We're not finished. But you don't have to do another day of it alone.

And just like that, she settled, not disappearing, not fading, but finding a kind of peace she hadn't had before.

Not as a wound.

As a witness.

To the truth she always deserved:

You were never the problem, sweetheart.

You were the beginning of a woman who would one day come back for you.

And here I am.

Chapter 19

How I Move Now
That I Trust Myself

I want to tell you what an ordinary Tuesday looks like now.

Not a milestone. Not a breakthrough. Not a moment I marked in a journal or called someone about.

Just Tuesday.

I wake up and I am not already bracing for something. I walk into rooms without scanning them first. Without cataloging the faces for signs of threat, without calculating how much of myself is safe to bring, without the low hum of *how am I landing, what do they think, am I too much, not enough, taking up the right amount of space.*

I just walk in.

I am still considerate. Still warm. Still the woman who never met a stranger and probably never will.

But I do what I want, when I want.

Without the obligation that used to shadow every yes. The kind of yes that wasn't really a choice, that was just fear wearing the costume of generosity.

Not long ago, a dear friend called me. A significant figure in the speaking world, someone I love and respect deeply, someone whose opinion of my gifts I take seriously.

She was putting together a speaking engagement in another country and she wanted me to join her as the business and personal development expert.

The old version of me would have found a way. Would have moved things around, made it work, said yes before I'd even finished processing the ask, because I love her, because I'm honored she thought of me, because saying no to someone you love about something they believe in feels like a small betrayal.

I told her I wasn't interested.

Politely. Gratefully. Without leaving room for negotiation.

She pushed back. Gently, lovingly, with the conviction of someone who genuinely believes in what she was offering. She told me this space is my gift. That I belong in those rooms. That I should consider it.

I didn't bend.

Not because she was wrong about my gifts. Not because I'm closed to speaking or closed to that room or closed to her.

But because I get to decide.

On my terms. In my time. Without obligation to anyone else's vision of who I should be, even a loving one, even a correct one.

I said thank you. I meant it. And I stayed no.

And it was okay.

The sky did not fall.

My friend still loves me.

And I went about my Tuesday.

People ask me what healing looks like on the other side.

I tell them the truth: I can't think of just one example. There are so many now.

That sentence used to be impossible for me to say.

For most of my life I could give you a precise accounting of every door I didn't walk through.

Every opportunity I redirected before it could reach me.

Every room I entered sideways, making myself smaller than the space required.

I remembered all of it.

The lunch table.

The redirect.

The parking lot prayer.

The Wheaties box I never earned because I kept handing the microphone to someone else.

I kept meticulous score of my own smallness.

But wholeness?

Wholeness I've lost count of.

And that—

that right there—

is what the other side of healing feels like.

Not a single triumphant moment.

A life so full of showing up that the showing up stops feeling like an event and starts feeling like just—Tuesday.

The inner voice that used to narrate my every move with suspicion

still shows up sometimes.

Old habits don't disappear.

They just lose their authority.

And when that voice arrives now—

are you sure, are you enough, what if they find out—

I recognize it the way you recognize an old neighbor
you no longer owe anything to.
I see you.
Not today.

I sat with all of this recently.
The full weight of it.
The whole arc from that pallet on a stranger's floor
to this page.
And I ugly cried.
Not the pretty kind.
The kind that comes from the oldest place in you—
when it feels safe enough to surface.
And when it passed—
you know what I said?
This is so cool.
Because it is.
Because I am here.
Because Little CeWyon made it.
Because the woman I needed when I was a girl
turned out to be me.

I can hold my father's failures and his love in the same hand
without either one crushing the other.
I can think of my mother throwing those slippers down the
stairs
and feel the grief of it and the tenderness of it
and the complicated, lifelong love of it
all at once.
I can sit with the girl in the bathroom stall,

the toddler on the pallet,
the child who watched the bus leave every morning,
and say to all of them—
I came back for you.
We made it.
Look at what we built.

Who does she think she is?
I used to hear that and shrink.
Pre-answer it with smallness before anyone could answer it
with cruelty.
I know who she is now.
She's the four-year-old who evaluated an environment,
found it disrespectful,
and walked herself home.
She's the girl who wrote a song in a bathroom stall
and then sang it in chorus
because her soul needed somewhere to put the truth.
She's the woman who put a shopping center schematic on a
vision board
and claimed a location before she knew which door would
open.
She's the one who negotiated a record
while her hands were shaking
and used one hand to steady the other
and signed anyway.
She's the one who carried secrets that would have shattered
people she loved—
carried them alone, for decades, out of love—
and then chose to put them on a page
so someone else wouldn't have to carry theirs alone.

She's the one who asked *what's wrong with me*
in a parking lot
until she was empty enough to hear a different question.
She's the one who followed that question
down every rabbit hole,
through every open tab,
past every book that confirmed what she was already finding—
all the way back to herself.
Every facet, finally visible. Every flame, still burning.
She is—
I am—
the woman I needed when I was a girl.
And here I am.

About the Author

CeWyon Chandler-Ward has been a firefighter, a beauty pageant queen, a professional cheerleader, and a licensed insurance agent. Every aptitude test pointed her toward leadership, entrepreneurship, coaching, and professional speaking, but every one of those paths required a level of self-worth she didn't yet possess. So she ran. Until she didn't.

Entrepreneurship runs deep in her veins, an undeniable legacy forged by generations of successful business operators. Armed with business degrees, she built multimillion-dollar enterprises, designed entrepreneurial curricula for prestigious institutions, and created hundreds of jobs within her community. Today, she anchors that drive as the operator of Hand & Stone Massage and Facial Spa in Decatur, Georgia.

Writing it, unearthing her steepest challenges and bearing her deepest vulnerabilities for the world to see, became undeniable evidence that the healing was real. She chose to narrate the audiobook herself, because some truths can only be spoken in your own voice.

The pearls she wears aren't decoration. They're a reminder that something painful can settle inside you, and instead of letting it destroy you, you can wrap it in layers of healing until it becomes the most beautiful thing you've ever produced.

Of all her accomplishments, the roles she guards most fiercely are wife and mother to two amazing young adult daughters. Residing near Atlanta, CeWyon now dedicates her life and her story to a single mission: ensuring that you never have to shrink to fit the spaces you were always meant to outgrow.

www.ingramcontent.com/pod-product-compliance
Lightning Source LLC
Chambersburg PA
CBHW041558160726

48006CB00042B/2062